The Far Left: Killing American Capitalism and Raising Socialism with More Enslavement of the Citizenry

Gaines Bradford Jackson, BS, MS, DrPH

THE FAR LEFT: KILLING AMERICAN CAPITALISM AND RAISING SOCIALISM WITH MORE ENSLAVEMENT OF THE CITIZENRY

iUniverse books may be ordered through booksellers or by contacting:

iUniverse
1663 Liberty Drive
Bloomington, IN 47403
www.iuniverse.com
844-349-9409

Because of the dynamic nature of the Internet, any web addresses or links contained in this book may have changed since publication and may no longer be valid. The views expressed in this work are solely those of the author and do not necessarily reflect the views of the publisher, and the publisher hereby disclaims any responsibility for them.

Any people depicted in stock imagery provided by Getty Images are models, and such images are being used for illustrative purposes only.
Certain stock imagery © Getty Images.

ISBN: 978-1-6632-4772-8 (sc)
ISBN: 978-1-6632-4775-9 (e)

Library of Congress Control Number: 2022921173

Print information available on the last page.

iUniverse rev. date: 05/05/2023

CONTENTS

ACKNOWLEDGMENTS

I have some significant acknowledgements to relate to the reader regarding people who played important roles in bringing this entire document to fruition.

The encouragement from my four children was most encouraging as they continually told me, "Yes, Daddy! You can do it. Just keep focused." Just those words were worth all the sweat, toil, and hours that went into compiling this document. I cannot forget the many hours that my editors spent correcting my typing errors, and to them I say a hardy "Thank you very much."

And finally, I am extremely grateful to the iUniverse book publishing company, which has pushed through the knowledge barrier and developed a straightforward and very professional publication process that has helped thousands of amateur authors recognize their own achievement potential.

PREFACE

R eaders will notice that each chapter of this labor of love starts out with a quote from one of the greatest presidents of the United States of America, Abraham Lincoln, to set a patriotic mood. This book was written to inform readers that a few selected far-left ideas of today's Democratic political party are simply *poison* for America, or any nation for that matter, as they would lead to mass demonstrations and active-shooter situations, in the mind of the author. Hopefully, reading this book will turn readers' minds away from the far left and back to the moderate right and rational sanity, smaller federal government, and peace and tranquility for the American people.

For example, the far left is bent on destroying capitalism and pushing for socialism, as they have lost sight of the following:

- One cannot bring about prosperity by discouraging thrift.
- One cannot strengthen the weak by weakening the strong.
- One cannot help the wage earner by pulling down the wage payer.
- One cannot further the community of humans by encouraging class hatred.
- One cannot help the poor by destroying the rich.
- One cannot keep out of trouble by spending more than one earns.
- One cannot build character and courage by taking away people's initiative and independence.
- One cannot help people permanently by doing for them what they could and should do for themselves. These words need to be echoed today for Abraham Lincoln originally spoke them in 1886. Is it not amazing how history repeats itself?

Following are items on the National Democratic Party's political agenda that we will discuss in this book:

1. More federal agencies are needed to quash state rights.
2. Implement a universal basic income (UBI) for all and legalize drugs (marijuana).
3. Defund the police (DTP).
4. Disallow all gun ownership.
5. Remove assault weapons and high-capacity magazines.
6. Pack the Supreme Court with left-minded judges by expanding the number of members.
7. Legitimize the LGBTQ+ community.
8. Do not support the grassroots movement for a twenty-eighth amendment.
9. CDC (big government) knows best regarding the control of bioweapons.
10. Instill open borders with no security.

The chapters of this labor of love are all designed to inform readers of exactly how insane this political agenda really is, and hopefully readers will follow up with communications to their political representatives and senators.

Chapter 1 explains to readers how governments can slowly and quietly enslave the citizenry, what the far-left philosophy is, and differences between capitalism and so-called democratic socialism.

Chapter 2 aids readers in understanding that the Democrats' platform tenet that the *bigger the government is, the better it is for society* is false and, in fact, the exact opposite is true. All government agencies need to be downsized on both the state and federal fronts to lower the cost of government operations and, in the long run, lower taxes.

Chapter 3 explains how the second item in the far-left agenda regarding *universal basic income and legalizing drugs* (in particular marijuana) in the long run is a secret mechanism to further enslave the citizenry.

Chapter 4 explains how *defunding the police (DTP)* is not only totally insane but opens the door for a rise in crime and potentially compelling mentally disturbed people to attempt more mass shootings. Remember that no gun ever killed anyone by itself, but mentally disturbed operators of guns kill others all the time.

Chapter 5 addresses how item four of the Democratic platform, *attempting to disallow gun ownership completely,* is also completely insane and constitutes borderline infringement on the rights in the Second Amendment. All Americans need to rise up against this idea. John Q. Citizen needs handguns and rifles for personal protection and for engaging in various sports activities (such as skeet shoots).

Chapter 6 delves into how item five of the Democratic platform, *banning assault rifles and high-capacity magazines from the general public,* might not be a bad idea if they leave handguns and rifles alone. It makes good sense to limit the availability of assault rifles, bump stocks, and high-capacity magazines to the military as these items are used only for killing people, one of the jobs reserved for the military.

Chapter 7 describes how *packing the Supreme Court* with additional far-left-minded justices is a terrible idea indeed. The present arrangement of eight justices and one chief justice, for a total of nine, seems to work quite well, and if something is working well, then do not mess with it.

Chapter 8 explains that item seven of the Democratic platform, regarding legitimizing *the LGBTQ+ community,* is to this author a fairly low form of a vote-getting mechanism. The individuals who comprise the LGBTQ+ community do have civil rights that deserve respect and protection, and others not of this community need to recognize this fact.

Chapter 9 details that item eight of the Democratic platform, *not supporting the grassroots movement for a twenty-eighth amendment,* is a horrible idea. The root of all evil in our present-day US government is the *career politician* and the *unregulated judiciary.* And as will be explained in the chapter, the components of the proposed twenty-eighth amendment are a partial and sane way of correcting the two major evils mentioned earlier.

Chapter 10 deals with the platform tenet that *CDC (big government) knows best regarding the control of bioweapons.* This turned out to be a major boondoggle if ever there was one. Big government failed miserably as politicians would never admit that the COVID-19 pandemic was really a bioweapon attack on the entire globe led by the Chinese, that testing for the virus had all kinds of problems, and that untested and unproven vaccines were mandated for the general public. Also, those recombinant mRNA vaccines could kill people whose immune systems were already compromised (such as diabetics). Many mistakes were made, and they are explained in this chapter. In retrospect, since we now know that it was a bioweapon attack, the military should have been involved from the outset.

Chapter 11 explains that the tenth item of the Democratic platform, *maintaining open borders with no security,* was a sorry way of attempting to build a voting database for their party. We should have wised up after 9/11 and realized that open borders are an extremely dangerous way to operate. No place in the whole world is safe, as we read of terrorist attacks happening somewhere every day.

Chapter 12 sums things up about the *crazy* Democratic party in general, with some ending discussions on *extremism* and *the fall of democratic types of government.* Further, the chapter discusses how the *2020 election in the United States was stolen electronically, coupled with universal balloting stuffing.*

CHAPTER 1

✳ ✳ ✳ ✳

INTRODUCTION

Let every American, every lover of liberty, every well-
wisher to his posterity, swear by the blood of the Revolution,
never to violate in the least particular, the laws of the
country; and never to tolerate their violation by others.

— Abraham Lincoln

To the readers of this book, please read the entire book to understand what the title means. If Mr. Biden and Ms. Harris succeed in implementing their socialist agenda, your freedoms and independence will be replaced with servitude to the federal government. John Q. Citizen will be forced to accept that Uncle Sam will take care of him with free education, free health care, and a guaranteed annual income. The hard truth is that there is no free education, no free universal health care, or anything guaranteed because someone, somewhere, pays down the line through an increase in federal income taxes. For example, health care for your family is not a right at all but a privilege and the responsibility of the breadwinner of each family, if he or she truly cares for his or her family.

Therefore, what can we expect from the progressive socialistic Democrats during the next few years? Here are fourteen signposts on the road to totalitarianism compiled some years ago by historian Dr. Warren Carroll and a refugee from Yugoslavian communism, Mike Djordjevich. The list is not in any particular order, but the imposition of any one of these new restrictions on liberty (none of which was in effect when the list was compiled) would be a clear warning that the totalitarian state is very near. And once a significant number of the signposts—perhaps five—have been imposed, we can rationally conclude that the remainder would not be far behind and that the fight for freedom and independence and the preservation of the republic has been lost in this country.

The Fourteen Signposts of Governmental Enslavement

1. Restrictions on taking money out of the country and on the establishment or retention of a foreign bank account by an American citizen
2. Abolition of private ownership of handguns
3. Detention of individuals without judicial process
4. Requirement that all private financial transactions be linked to social security numbers or other government identification in order that government records of these transactions can be kept in a computer database
5. Use of compulsory-education laws to forbid attendance at presently private schools
6. Compulsory nonmilitary service
7. Compulsory psychological treatment for nongovernment workers or public school children
8. An official declaration that anticommunist organizations are subversive and subsequent legal action taken to suppress them
9. Laws limiting the number of people allowed to gather in a private home irrespective of subject matter
10. Any significant change in passport regulations to make passports more difficult to obtain or use
11. Wage and price controls, especially in a nonwartime situation
12. Any kind of compulsory registration with the government regarding where individuals work
13. Any attempt to restrict freedom of movement within the United States
14. Any attempt to make a new major law by executive decree (that is actually put into effect, not merely authorized as by existing executive orders)[1]

As readers are no doubt aware, President Nixon invoked signposts 1, 11, and 14 according to historical records. Additionally, be aware of the fact that signposts 2, 3, 6, 9, 12, and 13 have already been proposed and Democrats are actively campaigning for them in organized democratic social-progressive groups. You might also want to be aware that, as of January 1, 1972, all American banks must report to the government any deposit or withdrawal over ten thousand dollars. The next step will be restricting the amount of money that can be taken out of country. People, the progressive Democrats are none other than Big Brother, watching your private bank account. (Does this not irritate you?)

Increasing government control over many kinds of private schools, as proposed by the Obama administration and annually in many state legislatures, is ongoing. Compulsory nonmilitary service is a universal draft of all young men and women, with a minority going into the armed services, and has been discussed by the Democratic party and Obama administration as an alternative to the draft. Sensitivity training is already required for an increasing number of government workers, teachers, and schoolchildren.

The so-called progressive Democratic party is counting on your being too preoccupied with your own problems or too lazy to fight back while the chains of slavery are being fastened on you. They are counting on their mass media influence to con you, frighten you, or ridicule you out of saving your freedom, and most of all, they are counting on your thinking you can escape by not taking part in opposing their secret takeover. They are also counting on those of you who are aware enough to recognize the Democratic party's conspiracy becoming so involved with watching all their moves that you become totally mesmerized by their machinations and thus incapable of acting. The choice is yours, but to this author it is quite clear that if one wishes to stop the transition to slavery, one should always vote Republican.[2-5]

What Is the Far Left?

Far-left politics are those further to the left on the left–right political spectrum than the standard political left. There are different definitions of the far left. Some scholars define it as representing the left side of social democracy, while others limit it to the left side of communist parties. In certain instances, especially in the news media, far-left thinking has been associated with some forms of authoritarianism, anarchism, and communism, and at times it characterizes groups that advocate for revolutionary socialism, Marxism and related communist ideologies, anticapitalism, or antiglobalization. Similar to far-right politics, extreme far-left politics can involve politically motivated violent acts, such as genocide and terrorism, as well as radicalization and the formation of far-left militant organizations. Far-left terrorism consists of militant or insurgent groups that attempt to realize their ideals and bring about change through political violence rather than through traditional political processes. In addition, governments ruled by political parties that either describe themselves or are identified by scholars as far-left have caused political repression, indoctrination, xenophobia, and mass killings. The definition of the far left varies in the literature, and there is not a general agreement on what it entails or consensus on the core characteristics that constitute it, other than being to the left of the political left. In France, *extrême-gauche* ("extreme left") is a generally accepted term for political groups that position themselves to the left of the Socialist Party, although some, such as the political scientist Serge Cosseron, limit the scope to the left of the French Communist Party.

Scholars such as Luke March and Cas Mudde propose that socioeconomic rights are at the far left's core. Moreover, March and Mudde argue that the far left is beyond the political left with regard to how parties or groups describe economic inequality on the basis of existing social and political arrangements. March, a senior lecturer in Soviet and post-Soviet politics and international relations of the University of Edinburgh, defines the far left as those who position themselves to the left of social democracy, which is seen as either insufficiently left wing or as defending the social-democratic tradition that is perceived to have been lost.

The two main subtypes of far-left politics are called the radical left and the extreme left; the first desires fundamental changes in neoliberal capitalism and progressive reform of democracy, such as direct democracy and the inclusion of marginalized communities, while the latter denounces liberal democracy as a "compromise with bourgeois political forces" and defines capitalism more strictly. Far-left politics is seen as radical politics because it calls for fundamental change to the capitalist socioeconomic structure of society.

March and Mudde say that far-left parties are increasingly stabilized political actors and are challenging mainstream social-democratic parties, defining other core characteristics of far-left politics as internationalist and focusing on networking and solidarity, as well as opposing globalization and neoliberalism. In his later conceptualization, March started to refer to far-left politics as radical left politics, which is composed of radical-left parties that reject the socioeconomic structures of contemporary society that are based on the principles and values of capitalism.[7–15]

Contrast Capitalism and Socialism

Capitalism is an economic system based on the private ownership of the means of production and their operation for profit. Central characteristics of capitalism include capital accumulation, competitive markets, price system, private property, property rights recognition, voluntary exchange, and wage labor. In a capitalist market economy, decision-making and investments are determined by owners of wealth, property, or ability to maneuver capital or production ability in capital and financial markets— whereas prices and the distribution of goods and services are mainly determined by competition in goods and services markets. Economists, historians, political economists, and sociologists have adopted different perspectives in their analyses of capitalism and have recognized various forms of it in practice. These include laissez-faire or free-market capitalism, state capitalism, and welfare capitalism. Different forms of capitalism feature varying degrees of free markets, public ownership, obstacles to free competition, and state-sanctioned social policies. The degree of competition in markets and the role of intervention and regulation as well as the scope of state ownership vary across different models of capitalism. The extent to which different markets are free and the rules defining private property are matters of politics and policy. Most of the existing capitalist economies are mixed economies that combine elements of free markets with state intervention and in some cases economic planning. Market economies have existed under many forms of government and in many different times, places, and cultures. Modern capitalist societies developed in Western Europe in a process that led to the Industrial Revolution. Capitalist systems with varying degrees of direct government intervention have since become dominant in the Western world and continue to spread. Economic growth is a characteristic tendency of capitalist economies.[16–21]

Socialism is a left-wing political, social, and economic philosophy encompassing a range of economic and social systems characterized by social ownership of the means of production, as opposed to private ownership. It includes the political theories and movements associated with such systems. Social ownership can be public, collective, or cooperative. While no single definition encapsulates the many types of socialism, social ownership is the one common element. Different types of socialism vary based on the role of markets and planning in resource allocation, on the structure of management in organizations, and from below or from above approaches, with some socialists favoring a party, state, or technocratic-driven approach. Socialists disagree on whether government, particularly existing government, is the correct vehicle for change. Socialist systems are divided into nonmarket and market forms. Nonmarket socialism substitutes factor markets and often money with integrated economic planning and engineering or technical criteria based on calculations performed in-kind, thereby producing a different economic mechanism that functions according to different economic laws and dynamics than those of capitalism. A nonmarket socialist system seeks to eliminate the perceived inefficiencies, irrationalities, unpredictability, and crises that socialists traditionally associate with capital accumulation and the profit system in capitalism. By contrast, market socialism retains the use of monetary prices, factor markets, and in some cases the profit motive with respect to the operation of socially owned enterprises and the allocation of capital goods between them. Profits generated by these firms would be controlled directly by the workforce of each firm or accrue to society at large in the form of a social dividend. Anarchism and libertarian socialism oppose the use of the state as a means to establish socialism, favoring decentralization above all, whether to establish nonmarket socialism or market socialism. Socialist politics has been both internationalist and nationalist; organized through political parties and opposed to party politics, at times overlapping with trade unions and at other times independent and critical of them, and present in both industrialized and developing nations. Social democracy originated within the socialist movement, supporting economic and social interventions to promote social justice. While retaining socialism as a long-term goal, since the postwar period it has come to embrace a Keynesian mixed economy within a predominantly developed capitalist market economy and liberal democratic polity that expands state intervention to include income redistribution, regulation, and a welfare state. Economic democracy proposes that a sort of socialist political movement includes a set of political philosophies that originated in the revolutionary movements of the mid- to late eighteenth century and out of concern for the social problems that were associated with capitalism. By the late nineteenth century, after the work of Karl Marx and his collaborator Friedrich Engels, socialism had come to signify opposition to capitalism and advocacy for a postcapitalist system based on some form of social ownership of the means of production. By the 1920s, communism and social democracy had become the two dominant political tendencies within the international socialist movement, with socialism itself becoming the most influential secular movement of the twentieth century. Socialist parties and ideas remain a political force with varying degrees of power and influence on all continents, heading national governments in many countries around the world. Today, many socialists have also adopted the causes of other social movements such as feminism, environmentalism, and progressivism. While the emergence of the Soviet Union as the world's first nominally socialist state led to socialism's widespread association with the Soviet economic model, some economists like Richard D. Wolff, and intellectuals like Noam Chomsky posit that, in practice, the model functioned as a form of state capitalism or an unplanned administrative or command economy. Several academics, political commentators, and scholars have distinguished between authoritarian socialist and democratic socialist states, with the first representing the Eastern Bloc and the latter representing Western Bloc countries, which have been democratically governed by socialist parties, such as Britain, France, Sweden, and Western countries in general, among others. However, following the end of the Cold War, many of these countries have moved away from socialism as a neoliberal consensus replaced the social democratic consensus in the advanced capitalist world.[22–25]

Summary

Now that you know some conceptual differences between capitalism and socialism, proceed to the next chapter to learn how the Democratic party is trying to implement socialistic items in their agenda and further enslave the American citizenry.

CHAPTER 2

✳ ✳ ✳ ✳

MORE FEDERAL AGENCIES ARE NEEDED TO QUASH STATE RIGHTS

Let every man remember that to violate the law is
to trample on the blood of his father, and to tear
the charter of his own and his children's liberty.

— Abraham Lincoln

The idea that larger federal government is most desirable and is more efficient than smaller federal government is totally wrong. In this chapter we will explore the pros and cons and hopefully convince the reader that the far-left belief that more government is needed actually breeds inefficiency and waste, as pointed out by the Brookings Institute. The author will present a hypothetical case that explains what happens in the real world.

Bigger versus Smaller

Let us face the truth: the big federal government failed miserably in the recent COVID-19 pandemic crisis. Also, the George W. Bush administration made a horrible mistake in going after Iraq rather than Saudi Arabia despite knowing that the hijackers in the 9/11 disaster were all Saudis. Additionally, there was no need to create the Homeland Security Agency. It was discovered later that the FBI did not coordinate or share information with the CIA. All that really happened was that the incompetent personnel of the FBI and CIA were retained, the HSA was created, and air travel became cumbersome—not smart at all.

Now let us list the possible pros and cons of expanding the federal government.

More Federal Government—Pros

- Greater regulation of potentially dangerous industries and market forces.
- Greater oversight of education system to ensure quality or more indoctrination
- Ability to enact more widespread social programs
- Much easier to carry out cover-ups of widespread corruption within government itself
- Greater ability to enforce rights
- Greater ability to oppress the citizenry over taxes
- Greater chance to enslave the citizenry

More Federal Government—Cons

- Can be stifling, particularly to those who cherish or fetishize freedom
- Higher operating costs, higher taxes, and more stress on the citizenry
- Less flexible, sometimes ridiculously so, leading to inefficiency
- Complex, often with overlapping mechanisms that can slow down the speed of operations due to redundancies
- Corruption more easily hid as well as being open to more opportunity
- Leads to many agencies doing the same thing, resulting in inefficiency
- Greater chance to hide fraud
- Becomes much harder to get rid of bad employees

Now we will list the pros and cons associated with downsizing the federal government:

Less Federal Government—Pros

- Greater flexibility *(in theory)*
- Lower operating costs (lower taxes)
- Less income tax harassment to fund pork projects
- Fewer personnel to corrupt or become corrupted
- Greater efficiency *(in theory)*
- Lowering of welfare rolls
- Enhanced waiting time to apply for welfare
- Encourages people to be more self-sufficient
- Recognizes state rights
- Lower overall taxes on the citizenry
- Generally makes it easier for people to own their own homes
- Creates less stress overall and make citizenry much happier

Less Federal Government—Cons

- Incapable of carrying out widespread social, economic, or political programs, even when needed, because not all states are on board
- Lack of personnel can hinder its operational efficiency, and adding more will require on-the-job training, which is ridiculously inefficient (especially for temporary employees)
- Likely would result in a lack of oversight and regulation in basic services, like health, education, and so on, resulting in a *highly* unequal panorama that varies by administrative region
- Decentralization of power likely leads to regionalism and possibly secessionism (the bane of human civilization)
- Less able to protect essential rights
- Lack of economic oversight capabilities likely result in a tumultuous market or a very monopolistic or oligopolistic one (the author suspects)[1]

A Hypothetical Case to Prove Big Government Inefficiency

Here is a hypothetical case to demonstrate just how inefficient most governmental agencies really are. Many have overlapping responsibilities, but none of their employees wish to stick their necks out, preferring instead to be quiet and draw a salary. Now, suppose you are a waste hauler along the Houston Ship Channel in the great state of Texas, and you have a three-thousand-gallon tanker truck in which you have collected waste from several industries. You have been paid up front to dispose of the stuff you have collected. You are aware that the medical waste you have in your tanker truck contains pathogens and some deadly anthrax spores, in addition to radioactive isotopes used in cancer research, volatile organic hydrocarbons that are potentially explosive, and waste cyanide and hydrogen sulfide, both of which are poisonous to humans when inhaled. Now, you are an honest, hard-working hauler and want to comply with all the rules and regulations. You must call the Department of Transportation (DOT) to get approval to carry hazardous waste across state borders, the Nuclear Regulatory Commission (NRC) to move possible radioactive waste, the Centers for Disease Control and Prevention (CDC) to move potentially deadly anthrax spores, and the Environmental Protection Agency (EPA) because they monitor hazardous waste from cradle to grave (because of the Resource Conservation and Recovery Act [RCRA]), and finally you must get approval from the Department of Defense (DOD) to move explosive material across state borders and through metropolitan areas. Now, you adhere to all the necessary safety procedures and get approval to move the waste to an abandoned mine shaft in the state of Kansas from DOT, DOD, NRC, and EPA but not the CDC. So now you have to go through the request process all over again and are so frustrated that you go to a far, remote section of Texas, find a two-lane dirt road (to achieve maximum absorption), open the stopcock on the tanker truck, and drain the waste out onto the road in the wee hours of the morning, hoping you will not get caught.

This scenario takes place over and over again because no single agency will stick its neck out to approve the transport of the waste, and just one disapproval from one of five agencies leaves haulers in limbo. What needs to be done is reducing the agencies—DOT, NRC, CDC, EPA, and DOD—in size and responsibility and creating a single Dangerous Substance Agency for multiple-matrix waste transportation (which is true with most industrial waste accumulations in the first place) for the waste haulers to make things much more efficient and boost their business in a safe and effective manner while cutting government's involvement down and saving taxpayers' money.[3]

Summary

All too often, this hypothetical case is true because of overlapping responsibilities and minions on the government dole who are too weak to make an accurate decision. Now, proceed to chapter three to learn the pros and cons of the far left's concept of *universal income for all and legalization of marijuana* (both enslavement programs).

CHAPTER 3

✳ ✳ ✳ ✳

UNIVERSAL BASIC INCOME FOR ALL AND LEGALIZING DRUGS

*At what point shall we expect the approach of danger? By
what means shall we fortify against it? Shall we expect
some transatlantic military giant, to step the Ocean,
and crush us at a blow? Never! All the armies of Europe,
Asia and Africa combined, with all the treasure of the
earth (our own excepted) in their military chest; with a
Buonaparte for a commander, could not by force, take a
drink from the Ohio, or make a track on the Blue Ridge,
in a trial of a thousand years. At what point, then, is the
approach of danger to be expected? I answer, if it ever
reach us it must spring up amongst us. It cannot come
from abroad. If destruction be our lot, we must ourselves
be its author and finisher. As a nation of freemen,
we must live through all time, or die by suicide.*

— Abraham Lincoln

Another idiotic far-left agenda item is to push for the legalization of
marijuana as a recreational drug and entice the citizenry to get money
automatically ever year with this *universal basic income* idea. The citizens
do not realize that both ideas are part of an insidious mechanism to enslave
them to the drug and the government for life.

Universal Basic Income Destroys Entrepreneurship

A universal basic income (UBI) is an unconditional cash payment given at regular intervals by the government to all residents, regardless of their earnings or employment status. Pilot UBI or more limited basic income programs that give a basic income to a smaller group of people instead of an entire population have taken place or are ongoing in Brazil, Canada, China, Finland, Germany, India, Iran, Japan, Kenya, Namibia, Spain, and the Netherlands as of October 20, 2020. In the United States, the Alaska Permanent Fund (AFP), created in 1976, is funded by oil revenues and provides dividends to permanent residents of the state. The amount varies each year based on the stock market and other factors and has ranged from $331.29 (1984) to $2,072 (2015). The payout for 2020 was $992.00, the smallest check amount since 2013. UBI has been in American news mostly thanks to the 2020 presidential campaign of Andrew Yang, whose continued promotion of a UBI resulted in the formation of a nonprofit called Humanity Forward.

We should at this time evaluate the pros and cons of a UBI.

Implementation of UBI—Pros

- Reduces poverty and income inequality and may improve physical and mental health
- May lead to positive job growth and lower school-dropout rates
- Guarantees income for nonworking parents and caregivers, thus empowering people in important traditionally unpaid roles, especially for women

Implementation of UBI—Cons

- Takes money from the poor and gives it to everyone, increasing poverty and depriving the poor of much-needed targeted support
- Is too expensive, as it is destined to increase over time, causing higher taxes
- Removes the incentive to work, adversely affecting the economy and leading to a labor and skills shortage

- Guaranteed to enhance welfare rolls
- Produces societal woes in a large population that has no shame[1]

According to Robert Greenstein, president of the Center on Budget and Policy Priorities, "If you take the dollars targeted on people in the bottom fifth or two-fifths of the population and convert them to universal payments to people all the way up the income scale, you're redistributing income upward. That would increase poverty and inequality rather than reduce them."[1] This makes rational sense to this author.

Destroys Incentives to Do Better and Enhances Enslavement

Medical marijuana is increasingly available in the United States as it is often used to treat chronic pain, muscle spasms, and nausea and vomiting, as well as to increase appetite. However, it can affect thinking and memory and increase the risk of accidents, and smoking it will harm the lungs and increase the risk of lung cancer, which in later stages is a death sentence. More than half of US adults, over 128 million people, have tried marijuana despite its being an illegal drug under federal law. Nearly six hundred thousand Americans are arrested for marijuana possession annually—more than one person per minute. Public support for legalizing marijuana went from 12 percent in 1969 to 66 percent today. Recreational marijuana, also known as adult-use marijuana, was first legalized in Colorado and Washington in 2012.[2,3]

Let us list the pros and cons of legalizing marijuana for further discussion purposes.

Legalize Marijuana—Pros

- Marijuana legalization boosts the economy.
- Legalizing marijuana results in decreased teen marijuana use.
- Traffic deaths and arrests for alcohol DUIs do not increase, and may decrease, when marijuana is legalized (just speculation).
- Legal marijuana is regulated for consumer safety.

- Legalization of marijuana phases out black markets and takes money away from drug cartels, organized crime, and street gangs.
- The enforcement of marijuana prohibition is racist because people of color are disproportionately impacted.
- Crime goes down when marijuana is legalized.
- Legalizing marijuana would end the costly enforcement of marijuana laws and free up police resources.
- Marijuana is less harmful than alcohol and tobacco, which are already legal (this is not totally true).
- Taxes collected from the legal sale of marijuana support important public programs.
- Legalizing marijuana creates thousands of needed jobs.
- A 2018 Gallup poll found that a majority of Americans support legalizing marijuana (66%).
- The government doesn't have the right to tell adults what they can put in their own bodies.

Legalize Marijuana—Cons

- Legalized marijuana creates steep costs for society and taxpayers that far outweigh its tax revenues.
- Legalizing marijuana increases use by teens, with harmful results.
- Legalizing marijuana increases traffic accidents.
- Marijuana is addictive, and dependence on the drug will increase with legalization.
- The black market and organized crime benefit from marijuana legalization.
- Legalizing marijuana leads to more marijuana-related medical emergencies.
- Marijuana use harms the brain, and legalization will increase mental health problems.
- Marijuana harms the health of users and people around them.
- Commercialized marijuana will create a "Big Marijuana" industry that exploits people for profit and targets children and teens.
- Legalizing marijuana hurts businesses by causing preventable accidents and lost productivity.

- The United States has signed international treaties that prevent us from legalizing marijuana.
- Legalizing marijuana is opposed by major public health organizations.
- Marijuana cultivation results in deforestation, soil erosion, habitat destruction, and river diversion.[4]

Rather than consume a lot of medical jargon on the ill effects of cannabis use, here is a quick abstract of an excellent book about marijuana, published in 2006.

The developing brain is susceptible to the effects of exogenous cannabinoids both during the perinatal period through maternal cannabis use and in young adolescent users. Emerging data from human and animal perinatal exposure studies demonstrate a subtle rather than gross effect of cannabis upon later functioning including; specific cognitive deficits especially in visuospatial function; impulsivity, inattention and hyperactivity; depressive symptoms; and substance use disorders. From animal studies motor control systems, neuroendocrine function and nociception may additionally be affected. Fetal studies indicate that these outcomes may be through cannabinoid mediated influences on the ontogeny of, especially dopamine and opioid, neurotransmitter systems. The effects of cannabinoids in the adolescent suggest long-term deleterious outcomes in cognition, depressive symptoms, schizophrenia and substance use disorders. Much of these data support a neurodevelopmental effect, however, predisposing genetic and/or environmental factors cannot be excluded from human studies. Gender specific differences have been observed in both human and animal studies implying sex hormone and related factors may interact with cannabinoids in neurodevelopment. Further understanding how cannabinoids influence neurodevelopment will inform public debate about the health effects of cannabis but also open avenues in discerning how *modulation of the endocannabinoid system may assist in the development of therapeutic tools for a variety of neuropsychiatric disorders.*[5-7] (emphasis added)

Summary

What the authors of this book are saying, in layperson's terms, is that long-term use of cannabis from adolescence to adulthood will cause a person to be lazy, irresponsible, unpunctual, unreliable, slow to learn, and overall lackadaisical. People with these lifelong characteristics will never be successful at any task they attempt to tackle in the near future. The goal of the far left is to ensure that all people wind up this way (brains flooded with dopamine and opioids) and UBI to ensure lifelong enslavement.

CHAPTER 4

✳ ✳ ✳ ✳

DEFUND THE POLICE

Determine that the thing can and shall be
done, and then we shall find the way.
— Abraham Lincoln

Totally Insane

According to Wikipedia,

> "Defund the Police" is a slogan that supports divesting funds from police departments and reallocating them to non-policing forms of public safety and community support, such as social services, youth services, housing, education, healthcare and other community resources particularly for poor people. Activists who use the phrase may do so with varying intentions; some seek modest reductions, while others argue for full divestment as a step toward the abolition of contemporary police services. Activists who support the defunding of police departments often argue that investing in community programs could provide a better crime deterrent for communities; funds would go toward addressing social issues (like poverty, homelessness, and mental disorders). Police abolitionists call for replacing existing police forces with other systems

of public safety, like housing, employment, community health, education, and other programs. The "Defund The Police" (DTP) slogan became common during the George Floyd protests starting in May 2020.[1]

Debunk DTP

This mischaracterization of the DTP movement is not based on fact but rather fear. Please allow the author to address seven common myths associated with the campaign to demonstrate that, while some have labeled it a radical movement, the DTP philosophy is based on well-researched, evidence-based positions. We will debunk the movement.

Myth #1: *Defund means abolish.* One of the most misleading critiques of the movement is that *defund* means *abolish.* Opponents claim the movement undermines public safety through its efforts to end policing. The truth: the movement seeks to demilitarize police departments and reallocate funding to trained mental health workers and social workers to reduce unnecessary violent encounters between police and citizens. At least thirteen cities in the United States have currently engaged in policy programs to defund the police.

Myth #2: *Defunding will lead to disorder.* Another misconception is that police forces are what maintains order. However, studies have found that the best tools to establish peaceful societies are equity in education and infrastructure. Indeed, research shows that lack of education and illiteracy are some of the most significant predictors of future prison populations.

Myth #3: *Police protect the public from violence.* Critics of the police movement assert that we need heavily funded and armed police forces to protect the public from violent criminal elements. However, there isn't sufficient data to support that position. In fact, research has found that the police don't have a notoriously efficient track record of solving violent crime. Further, what the research does show is that 70 percent of robberies, 66 percent of rapes, 47 percent of aggravated assaults, and 38 percent of murders go unsolved each year. (Author's note: This is probably due to inefficient departments in general.)

Myth #4: *Community programs won't work.* While much of the available research contradicts the narrative that policing is essential to eliminating crime, substantial evidence shows that investing, developing, and supporting education and economic programs do, in fact, lead to fewer offenses and create more social harmony. Education has long been viewed as the great equalizer. Data supports the position that individuals who receive a quality education are less likely to become involved in the criminal justice system.

Myth #5: *Most police work is focused on crime prevention.* There is minimal evidence that police surveillance results in reduced crime or prevents crime. For instance, research showed that 90 percent of the people that were stopped in the NYPD's controversial stop-and-frisk program were not committing any crime. While it is true that police do apprehend individuals who violate the law, this is just one of several components of their responsibilities. (Author's note: such as being community stewards.)

Myth #6: *Police officers do not need college degrees.* Research clearly demonstrates that police officers who have at least two years of a college education are less likely to have misconduct complaints and less likely to use force to gain compliance. And officers with only high school diplomas account for 75 percent of disciplinary problems. The evidence shows that reform efforts should not ignore the application pool crisis and law enforcement departments should instill more robust higher education standards.

Myth #7: *Defunding the police is a fear-mongering reaction with no research.* Some opponents of cutting police budgets view the movement as an emotional response to police misconduct rather than a well-thought-out campaign. However, a study with sixty years of data indicates that increases in spending do not reduce crime. Which begs the question, how is sixty years of a failed objective any better? Yes, the movement gained attention because of tragic events in 2020, but the evidence supporting the movement is not based on hard data and proven methods. Police reform is probably long overdue, and we have had thousands of opportunities to make the appropriate changes. In 2020, the murder of George Floyd garnered national attention that has caused many to take a long, hard look at our democratic systems, cultural identities, and the necessary steps toward equal protection. We do know that more traditional policing may not be the answer.[2,3]

Encourages Crime and Mayhem

The simple facts are that crime and mayhem will increase when the crooks know that fewer police officers are on the beat watching their every move. Even those mentally challenged individuals thinking of committing a random mass shooting will think that they just might survive with fewer police on the response team. No matter what we choose to call it—defund the police, a reallocation of funding, or a total reimagination—research supports a public-health approach to policing. If we are effective, funding public health approaches will reduce the reliance on law-and-order policing, save lives, and reverse the longstanding slide in the wrong direction. Police must be the last resort, used only when necessary to protect the public from harm. Until then, municipalities will need to prepare for the impact of increased police accountability and transparency. Ultimately, the rising costs associated with police misconduct will force police reform, a cost that would have been much cheaper had we listened to those groups most impacted by aggressive policing. To see real change in our society, policymakers must remove the barriers and fund necessary programming. We need not raise taxes. We simply need to be smart and follow the science.

Summary

By now all Americans should realize that a responsive and smart police force is necessary to maintain peace and order and to respond to mass shootings in the quickest manner possible to reduce deaths as much as possible. Now, proceed to the next chapter to learn why removing individual gun rights is a bad idea.

CHAPTER 5

✳ ✳ ✳ ✳

REMOVE GUN OWNERSHIP PERIOD

The people—the people—are the rightful masters
of both congresses and courts—not to overthrow the
Constitution, but to overthrow the men who pervert it.
—Abraham Lincoln

According to Wikipedia, *gun control* means "the set of laws or policies that regulate the manufacture, sale, transfer, possession, modification, or use of firearms by civilians." Most countries have a restrictive firearm guiding policy, with only a few legislations being categorized as permissive. Jurisdictions that regulate access to firearms typically restrict access to only certain categories of firearms and then to restrict the categories of persons who will be granted a license to have access to a firearm. In some countries such as in the United States, gun control may be legislated at either a federal level or a local state level. Gun control refers to domestic regulation of firearm manufacture, trade, possession, use, and transport, specifically with regard to the class of weapons referred to as small arms (revolvers and self-loading pistols, rifles, and carbines, assault rifles, submachine guns, and light machine guns). Usage of the term *gun control* is sometimes politicized. Some of those in favor of legislation instead prefer to use terms such as *gun-violence prevention, gun safety, firearms regulation, illegal guns*, or *criminal access to guns*. For example, in 2007, it was estimated that globally there were about 875 million small arms in the hands of civilians, law enforcement agencies, and armed forces. Of these firearms 650 million, or 75 percent, are held by civilians. US civilians account for 270 million of this total. A further 200 million are controlled by state military forces. Law enforcement agencies have some 26 million small arms. Nonstate armed groups have about 1.4 million firearms. Finally, gang members hold between 2 and 10 million small arms. Together, the small arms arsenals of nonstate armed groups and gangs account for, at most, 1.4 percent of the global total.[1]

Many Americans support the right to bear arms but also believe that the government has the right to regulate firearms in the interest of public safety. Though there are differences along party lines, a 2021 Pew Research poll found that 53 percent of Americans believe gun control laws should be more strict, and 14 percent believe they should be less strict. Gun rights groups, such as the National Rifle Association (NRA), aim to prevent new gun control legislation and, if possible, roll back existing legislation. In the late twentieth century, the NRA began to wield significant political influence at the national and state levels, especially among conservative politicians. In response, gun control advocacy organizations such as Brady, Giffords, and Everytown for Gun Safety have worked to enact legislation designed to better regulate gun ownership, such as requiring waiting periods, background checks, gun permits, gun safety training, and restrictions on the possession of assault weapons.[2]

The Second Amendment

The right to keep and bear arms is included as the Second Amendment to the US Constitution as part of the Bill of Rights, ratified on December 15, 1791. It states: "A well Regulated Militia, being necessary to the security of a free State, the right of the people to keep and bear Arms, shall not be infringed." The precise meaning and purpose of the Second Amendment have been subjects of frequent debate in the early twenty-first century. At the time it was enacted, each state maintained a militia composed of ordinary, everyday citizens (farmers, shopkeepers, doctors, lawyers, and maybe blacksmiths) who served as part-time soldiers to protect settlers on land contested by Native Americans and defend against any attacks by foreign entities, some of which still held territories later claimed by the United States. In addition, some of the authors of the Second Amendment feared the federal government would use its standing army to force its will on the states and intended to protect the state militias' right to take up arms against the federal government. The author of this book believes that all law-abiding citizens have a right to bear handguns to protect their families and homesteads from unwanted intruders.

Opponents of so-called gun control, however, still interpret the Second Amendment as guaranteeing individual citizens' right to keep and bear arms. They assert the amendment protects the rights of the general population because colonial law required every household to possess arms and every white male of military age to be ready for self-defense and military emergencies. Therefore, by guaranteeing arms for the militia, the amendment simultaneously guaranteed arms for every citizen. Opponents of gun control further maintain the term "right of the people" in the Second Amendment holds the same meaning as it does in the First Amendment, which guarantees such individual liberties as the freedom of religion and freedom of assembly.

Proponents of gun control are now debating some of these interpretations and argue that much has changed since the amendment was written. Some twenty-first-century gun control supporters argue the amendment was meant to protect only a state's right to arm citizens for the common defense, not private citizen's rights to possess and carry any firearm in any space. They also argue that, according to the amendment, such militias were "well regulated," meaning they were subject to state requirements concerning training, firearms, and periodic military exercises. Hopefully wise individuals will see through this irrational thinking. [2,3]

Modern-Day Legal Development on Gun Control

The US Congress has created laws regarding gun regulations and the Supreme Court has ruled on several cases. The National Firearms Act (NFA) of 1934 was the country's first major federal gun control legislation. The law required the registration of certain firearms, imposed taxes on the sale and manufacture of firearms, and restricted the sale and ownership of high-risk weapons, such as machine guns. The Federal Firearms Act (FFA) of 1938 provided additional regulations, requiring federal licenses for firearm manufacturers and dealers and prohibiting certain people from buying firearms. The Supreme Court's ruling in *United States v. Miller* (1939) upheld the NFA and set a precedent that the right to bear arms applied to citizens in active, controlled state guard or militia units.

The next major piece of federal firearms legislation was the Gun Control Act (GCA) of 1968, passed in the wake of the assassinations of Dr. Martin Luther King Jr. and Senator Robert F. Kennedy. The GCA expanded both the NFA and the FFA. The law ended mail-order sales of all firearms and ammunition and banned the sale of guns to minors, felons, fugitives from justice, people who use illegal drugs, persons with mental illness, and those dishonorably discharged from the armed forces. The Supreme Court bolstered controls when it upheld New Jersey's strict gun control law in *Burton v. Sills* (1969) and the federal ban on possession of firearms by felons in *Lewis v. United States* (1980).

The Firearms Owners' Protection Act of 1986 (FOPA), however, eased many GCA restrictions. Opponents of gun control lauded FOPA for expanding where firearms could be sold and who could sell them but continued to object to prohibitions on the manufacture and possession of machine guns for civilian use. In 1989 the administration of President George H. W. Bush announced a permanent ban on importing assault rifles. With passage of the Public Safety and Recreational Firearms Use Protection Act of 1994 (also called the Federal Assault Weapons Ban), Congress banned the manufacture and sale of specific assault weapons. The ban expired in 2004.

The Brady Handgun Violence Prevention Act of 1993 passed as an amendment to the GCA. The Brady Act addressed several key concerns of gun control proponents by requiring a five-day waiting period for all handgun sales, during which a background check would be run on all prospective purchasers. This provision expired in 1998 and was replaced by the National Instant Criminal Background Check System (NICS), a database used to verify the eligibility of a buyer to possess a firearm.

Legislation and Court Cases in the Early Twenty-First Century

After several victims and families of victims of gun violence and others sued gun manufacturers and dealers whose weapons were used to commit a crime, Congress passed the Protection of Lawful Commerce in Arms Act (PLCAA) and the Child Safety Lock Act of 2005. The first act limited the liability of gun manufacturers and dealers when their firearms were used in crimes. The second act required anyone licensed to transfer or sell firearms to provide gun storage or safety devices. During his 2020 campaign for president, Democratic candidate Joe Biden supported repeal of the PLCAA.

Congress enacted the NICS Improvement Amendments Act in 2007. It was meant to improve failures in the NICS system that allowed a shooter to acquire a gun despite a disqualifying mental health status which was not submitted to NICS by the state of Virginia. He killed thirty-two people and himself on a Virginia college campus.

Gun rights proponents have used legislation as well as the federal courts to challenge gun restrictions. The US Supreme Court ruled in *District of Columbia v. Heller* (2008) that the Second Amendment prohibits the federal government from making it illegal for private individuals to keep loaded handguns in their homes. It was the first Supreme Court decision to explicitly rule that the right to keep and bear arms is an individual right. The Court's decision also clarified that the Second Amendment allows for limits on the types of arms that can be kept and how they are used. The Heller decision has been used as the basis for several city, county, and state bans on assault weapons and specific arms such as the AR-15 rifle.

State and local laws regarding licensing, registration, and possession of firearms vary widely. For instance, in some states a permit to carry a concealed weapon in public is only issued if the applicant demonstrates a need and is found to have the capacity to safely and responsibly handle firearms. In other states a concealed carry permit is guaranteed to any citizen legally allowed to own a weapon. As of January 2022, twenty-one states allowed concealed carry without a permit. Several courts have used the Heller decision as a basis to allow concealed carry of firearms.

Loopholes in Legislation that Has Been Presented to Date

Gaps in legislation can enable people to obtain guns who may not otherwise meet the legal requirements for purchase. The background check requirement, for example, can be avoided by purchasing firearms from an unlicensed seller who does not perform these checks. While referred to as the "gun show loophole," such sales can take place elsewhere, including online. Temporary loans of firearms are typically allowed as are transfers of weapons that are inherited or given as gifts. While unlicensed gun transfers are acceptable within one's own state, interstate sales are prohibited.

Federal law and some states allow juveniles to purchase long guns, such as rifles and shotguns, from an unlicensed firearms dealer. Child safety advocates have long campaigned for federal legislation that would raise the minimum age to own any type of firearm and have also called for regulations aimed at preventing children from accessing guns in the home.

An amendment passed in 1996 known as the Lautenberg Amendment prevents people who have been convicted of domestic abuse or are the subject of a protective order prohibiting contact from owning guns. However, abusers who are not a parent, guardian, or legal spouse to their victims face no such restrictions. This gap has become known as the "boyfriend loophole."

Underreporting and underfunding have contributed to the NICS database lacking substantial data in many categories. Lapses in NICS reporting resulted in multiple instances of sales of weapons to unauthorized persons who then used the weapons to commit crimes. For example, a former member of the US Air Force legally purchased a firearm and killed twenty-six people at a church in Sutherland Springs, Texas. Following the shooting, the Air Force acknowledged that they failed to report the shooter's military court martial conviction for domestic violence to civilian authorities. In response, Congress passed the Fix NICS Act of 2017 to penalize federal agencies that do not meet NICS reporting requirements.

In 2015 a gunman shot and killed nine Black worshippers at a Charleston, South Carolina, church. Authorities later discovered the perpetrator had purchased the murder weapon while still undergoing a background check. Sellers are allowed to give a buyer the weapon if the check takes more than three days. The House of Representatives passed a bill in 2021 to extend background checks from three days to ten days, allowing more time for a full check to be completed. Known as the "Charleston loophole" bill, as of January 2022 the Senate had not voted on the legislation.[2–4]

Summary

In light of new gun laws, it would behoove us all to ask the following critical thinking questions:

- Do you interpret the text of the Second Amendment to allow for an individual or a collective right to own weapons? Explain your reasoning.
- Do you agree with Supreme Court rulings establishing that the Second Amendment allows for certain gun control measures? Why or why not?
- In your opinion, are existing gun control regulations sufficient to ensure public safety? What other types of measures, if any, do you think are needed, and why?

Who knows what if any changes in the US gun laws will take place. As of the writing of this book, Congress is still debating what the new laws will be. One should consider that high-capacity magazines and assault rifles are war instruments, and new laws need to be put in place to restrict their accessibility to the general public in an effort to reduce mass killings in the homeland. Now, proceed to the next chapter to learn the pros and cons of high-capacity magazines and assault weapons.

CHAPTER 6

✳ ✳ ✳ ✳

REMOVE ASSAULT WEAPONS AND HIGH-CAPACITY MAGAZINES

*I do not mean to say that this government is
charged with the duty of redressing or preventing
all the wrongs in the world; but I do think that
it is charged with the duty of preventing and
redressing all wrongs which are wrongs to itself.*

— Abraham Lincoln

Pros and Cons of Banning Assault Weapons

First of all, we should list the pros and cons of what would probably happen if high-capacity magazines and assault weapons were banned.

Banning Assault Weapons and High-Capacity Magazines—Pros

- Though many gun-rights proponents state that guns are necessary for self-defense and hunting, such activities do not require the efficiency and firepower of automatic weapons and high-capacity ammunition magazines.
- Assault weapons are known to be capable of injuring and killing large groups of people in mass shootings, so banning them may reduce the number of casualties.

- Most Americans support a federal ban on military-style assault weapons.
- For politicians in many jurisdictions, supporting such legislation would reflect the will of the people.
- While the accidental discharge of a firearm always carries the risk of injury, the accidental discharge of an automatic weapon can result in much greater damage.

Banning Assault Weapons and High-Capacity Magazines—Cons

- Banning any type of firearm would be interpreted by some as a violation of the Second Amendment of the US Constitution.
- Because federal law forbids the importation of foreign-made assault weapons, all such weapons sold legally are manufactured domestically, thus helping local economies and encouraging further innovation. Banning them would hurt these areas.
- A federal assault weapons ban would have minimal impact on gun deaths, as the majority of gun deaths are self-inflicted and do not involve automatic weapons.[1]

Leave Handguns, Sport Rifles, and Shotguns Alone

With all the hype about mass shootings and all the human suffering afterward, it is likely that banning high-capacity magazines and assault guns such as the AR-15 will gain enough support that certain congresspeople will be forced to do so for the average John Q. Citizen in the United States of America. What people lose sight of however, that no assault rifle killed anyone by itself. The fact of the matter is that mental illness among the common, everyday citizenry is on the rise due to media blitzes, movies with lots of violence, violent videos watched on smartphones, violent video games, and even the national news, as it is mostly about violence. This continuous bombardment is turning rational people into raving maniacs, and this manifests in the form of mass shootings. Not to mention that, because the economy is in the pits, most people live off credit that they will never completely pay back, services and goods are in short supply, the far-left agenda to defund the police just increases the overall crime rate, and with all this going on, the overall enslavement to the government rises.

Summary

All citizens need to keep in mind that, if the government does ban high-capacity magazines and assault rifles, the door will be opened for them to go after handguns, sport rifles, and shotguns in the future unless something is specifically stated in the law that these items *must be left alone*. Now, proceed to the next chapter to learn what it means to "pack" the Supreme Court.

CHAPTER 7

✳ ✳ ✳ ✳

PACK THE SUPREME COURT WITH LEFT-MINDED JUDGES BY EXPANSION OF MEMBERS

Why should there not be a patient confidence
in the ultimate justice of the people? Is there
any better or equal hope in the world?

— Abraham Lincoln

The number of justices on the Supreme Court went up and down in the mid-1800s, at one time reaching ten members. In 1869 the number was set at nine and has stayed at nine since. President Franklin Delano Roosevelt tried to add members to the court in the 1930s, proposing to reorganize the court by adding a new justice each time an existing justice reached age seventy and did not retire. Congress failed to go along with FDR.

In the wake of President Trump's decision to put forth a nominee to fill Ruth Bader Ginsburg's seat on the US Supreme Court, some Democrats in Congress, angered at the timing of the move, have called for a change in the nation's highest court out of spite. Over fears that the institution will lean strongly to the right, potentially for thirty or forty years, Democrats have threatened to change the ideological complexion of the court by expanding the number of justices who hear the nation's top cases. Called "court packing," the issue made its way to the forefront of the presidential election with Democratic nominee Joe Biden and his running mate Sen.

Kamala Harris, D-California, being asked about it in debates and on the campaign trail. To pack the court means to add judges to a court. The US Supreme Court is made up of nine justices, with one of those justices being the chief justice. Democrats have not said how many justices they would consider adding if they got the chance. The Constitution does not specify how many justices are to sit on the Supreme Court. Originally, six justices served on the Supreme Court. That number changed several times, but in 1869, Congress decided to set the number at nine justices. If the House, the Senate, and the president agree, the number can be changed by passing a law. It would take a simple majority vote in both chambers for the bill to pass, and the president would have to sign it into law.[1]

Judicial Procedures Reform Bill of 1937

The Judicial Procedures Reform Bill of 1937, frequently called the court-packing plan, was a legislative initiative proposed by US president Franklin D. Roosevelt to add more justices to the US Supreme Court in order to obtain favorable rulings regarding New Deal legislation that the court had ruled unconstitutional. The central provision of the bill would have granted the president power to appoint an additional justice to the US Supreme Court, up to a maximum of six, for every member of the court over the age of seventy years. In the Judiciary Act of 1869, Congress had established that the Supreme Court would consist of the chief justice and eight associate justices. During Roosevelt's first term, the Supreme Court struck down several New Deal measures as being unconstitutional. Roosevelt sought to reverse this by changing the makeup of the court through the appointment of new additional justices who he hoped would rule that his legislative initiatives did not exceed the constitutional authority of the government. Since the US Constitution does not define the Supreme Court's size, Roosevelt believed it was within the power of Congress to change it. Members of both parties viewed the legislation as an attempt to stack the court, and many Democrats, including Vice President John Nance Garner, opposed it. The bill came to be known as Roosevelt's "court-packing plan," a phrase coined by Edward Rumely.[2]

Packing the Supreme Court Pros and Cons

The contemporary debate has been heavily influenced by events following the February 13, 2016, death of conservative associate justice Antonin Scalia. Citing the upcoming 2016 election, Senate Majority Leader Mitch McConnell (R-KY) refused to consider President Barack Obama's liberal Supreme Court nominee, Merrick Garland. At the time, there were 342 days remaining in Obama's presidency, 237 days until the 2016 election, and neither the 2016 Democratic nor Republican nominee had been chosen. Because the Senate approval process was delayed until 2017, the next president, Donald Trump, was allowed to appoint a new justice (conservative Neil Gorsuch) to what many Democrats called a "stolen seat" that should have been filled by Obama. The court-packing debate was reinvigorated in 2019 with the appointment of conservative associate justice Brett Kavanaugh by President Trump after liberal-leaning swing vote associate justice Anthony Kennedy retired in July 2018. In the wake of this appointment, South Bend, Indiana, mayor Pete Buttigieg, then also a 2020 presidential candidate, suggested expanding the court to fifteen justices in the October 15, 2019, Democratic presidential debate. Then largely brushed aside as "radical," the topic resurfaced once again upon the death of liberal stalwart associate justice Ruth Bader Ginsburg on September 18, 2020. Liberals, and some conservatives, argued that the 2016 precedent should be followed and that Justice Ginsburg's seat should remain empty until after the 2020 presidential election or the January 2021 presidential inauguration. However, McConnell and the Republicans in control of the Senate, and thus the approval process, indicated they would move forward with a Trump nomination without delay. McConnell defended these actions by stating the president and the Senate are of the same party (which was not the case in 2016, negating—from his perspective—that incident as a precedent that needed following), and thus the country had confirmed Republican rule. Others argued as well that, since there was a chance that the results of the 2020 election could be challenged in the courts, and perhaps even at the Supreme Court level (due to concerns over the handling of mail-in ballots and use of universal ballots), it was critical for an odd number of justices to sit on the court (for an even number, such as eight, could mean a split four-four decision on the critical question of who would be deemed the next US president, sending the country into a constitutional crisis). At the time of McConnell's September 18 announcement via Twitter, there were 124 days left in Trump's term and 45 days until the 2020 election. Some have called the impending nomination to replace Ginsburg and the 2016–2017 events a version of court packing by Republicans. Supreme Court nominees can be confirmed by the US Senate with a simple majority vote (as stated before), with the vice president called in to break a fifty-fifty tie. Amy Coney Barrett was confirmed by the Senate on October 26, 2020, with a fifty-two-to-forty-eight vote to replace Justice Ginsburg, eight days before the 2020 election.

Packing the Supreme Court—Pros

- The Supreme Court is politically partisan and ideologically imbalanced. Adding justices would ensure that it never reflects only one party's political agenda.
- Historical precedent allows for more than nine Supreme Court justices, and there are no laws against having more than nine.

Packing the Supreme Court—Cons

- The Supreme Court is largely balanced. Court packing would increase political interference in an independent branch of government. It's a slippery slope that would allow each president to add justices for rank political reasons.
- Historical precedent most strongly supports a nine-judge Supreme Court.[3]

Summary

Representative Jim Jordan (R-Ohio) was irritated at the Democrats' threats to expand the court, and he therefore submitted a resolution to Congress that would limit the court to nine justices: "Any attempt to increase the number of Justices of the Supreme Court of the United States or 'pack the court' would undermine our democratic institutions and destroy the credibility of our nation's highest court," the resolution reads. This whole idea of packing the court is nothing other than political party bricking. If the system is working fine, then do not mess with it.

Now we are ready to proceed to the next chapter and learn why the Democratic political party supports the LGBTQ+ community whole-heartedly.

CHAPTER 8

✳ ✳ ✳ ✳

LEGITIMIZE THE LGBTQ+ COMMUNITY

*It is as much the duty of government to render prompt
justice against itself, in favor of citizens, as it is to
administer the same between private individuals.*
— Abraham Lincoln

The believers in the far-left agenda will seek any avenue that they consider to have a large voting base to just get votes. This is why they champion themselves as being a staunch supporters of the human rights and civil rights of those in the LGBTQ+ community in general.

What Is the LGBTQ+ Community?

According to Wikipedia, the LGBTQ+ community (also known as the GLBT community, gay community, or queer community) is a loosely defined grouping of lesbian, gay, bisexual, transgender, and other queer individuals united by a common culture and social movements. These communities generally celebrate pride, diversity, individuality, and sexuality. LGBTQ+ activists and sociologists see such community building as a counterweight to heterosexism, homophobia, biphobia, transphobia, heterosexualism, and conformist pressures that exist in the larger norms of society. The term *pride* or sometimes *gay pride* expresses the LGBTQ+ community's identity and collective strength; pride parades provide both a prime example of the use and a demonstration of the general meaning of the term. The LGBTQ+ community is diverse in political affiliation. Not all people who are lesbian, gay, bisexual, or transgender consider themselves part of the LGBTQ+ community. Groups that may be considered part of this community include gay villages, LGBTQ+ rights organizations, employee groups at companies, student groups in schools and universities, and affirming religious groups. LGBTQ+ communities may organize themselves into or support movements for civil rights, promoting LGBTQ+ rights in various places around the world. As a matter of fact, in some Muslim cultures, members of the LGBTQ+ community are condemned to death by stoning.[1]

The facts are that the sexuality demonstrated by the LGBTQ+ community can be traced way back to the old Baal religion against which Jesus Christ preached, and even today these people are considered deviants from societal norms. They have lost sight of the fact that when Adam asked for a helpmate, he got an *Eve* and not a *Steve*. Let us now explore the question, "Why recognize the LGBTQ+ community when, in the past, it was around but was not widely known or was always behind closed doors?"

Societal Deviants' Recognition

The Democratic party's platform knows that people around the world face violence and inequality—sometimes torture and even execution—because of who they love, how they look, or who they are. Sexual orientation and gender identity are integral aspects of our selves and should never lead to discrimination or abuse and death. Their platform (they claim) works for lesbian, gay, bisexual, and transgender people's rights and with activists representing a multiplicity of identities and issues. They document and expose abuses based on sexual orientation and gender identity worldwide, including torture, killing and executions, arrests under unjust laws, unequal treatment, censorship, medical abuses, discrimination in health and jobs and housing, domestic violence, abuses against children, and denial of family rights and recognition. They go on to advocate for laws and policies that will protect everyone's dignity and work for a world where all people can enjoy their rights fully. However, the subtle goal is to get people to jump on the bandwagon for votes.[2]

Summary

Everyone has a right to his or her opinion on sexuality. The problems occur when the LGBTQ+ community thinks that it can force others in society to accept them, regardless of what those others think, by making a lot of unwanted noise. However, out of respect for others and to create societal harmony with those who think that the LGBTQ+ community is outside the norm, we still need to respect their civil liberties by practicing the following:

- **Do not** repeat or acknowledge anti-LGBT messages. For example, when opponents claim that gay people are trying to "destroy heterosexual marriage," don't respond by saying, "Gay couples are not destroying marriage." While it's tempting to argue against the false claims of antigay activists, repeating their language and sound bites (even to dispute them) just makes their concepts stick in people's minds. If repeating antigay language is unavoidable, think about using the so-called qualifier to remind audiences that opponents' terminology is false and misleading (e.g., "This so-called Defense of Marriage Act is really about hurting loving, committed couples").

- **Do not** use highly charged language. Research shows that using terms like "bigotry," "prejudice," and "hatred" to describe anti-LGBTQ+ attitudes is viewed by many Americans as shrill, confrontational name-calling. Attacking anti-LGBTQ+ activists doesn't give Americans a reason to support equality for LGBTQ+ people; rather, it can make them want to back away from the person or group doing the name calling. Instead, use language that is measured and relatable to create empathy and a sense of how opponents' attitudes and actions hurt LGBTQ+ people.

- **Do not** inadvertently validate anti-LGBTQ+ attitudes. Saying "I understand how talking about these issues can be challenging"—which lets someone know that you understand how difficult these discussions can sometimes be—is different from saying "I understand why you are opposed to this issue." Acknowledge the discomfort, not the person's hurtful attitudes.

- **Do not** compare—directly or indirectly—the experiences of gay and transgender people with those of African Americans, Latinos, or the immigrant rights movement. Likewise, do not make comparisons to the African American Civil Rights Movement. Research is clear: such comparisons alienate these audiences, and they don't actually help people understand the harms and injustices that LGBTQ+ people face.
- **Do not** use the language of conflict. Most Americans do not typically respond well to framing LGBTQ+ issues as a "war," "battle," or "fight." Avoid war metaphors and similar language. Instead, talk about the injustices that LGBTQ+ people experience on a daily basis and the importance of ensuring that all people— including LGBTQ+ people—are treated fairly and equally.

One must keep in mind that there are only two reasons why people grow up that way—either environmental influences or physical shortcomings in one's hormone levels as they migrate from adolescence to adulthood.[3]

Now we are ready to proceed to the next chapter and learn what the Twenty-Eighth Amendment movement is all about and why Democrats are dead set against its support and possible passage.

CHAPTER 9

✳ ✳ ✳ ✳

DO NOT SUPPORT THE GRASS ROOTS MOVEMENT FOR THE TWENTY-EIGHTH AMENDMENT

The people's will, constitutionally expressed,
is the ultimate law for all.

— Abraham Lincoln

The main corrupters of the American form of government are the *career politician and unregulated judiciary.* Why make such a rash statement? Well, allow me some of your time for an adequate explanation. Over two hundred years ago, Thomas Jefferson made the statement, "Politicians should serve one term as public servants then go back home and go to work." What he meant by that statement was that public servants should not become career politicians and suck off the government all their lives. It is quite evident today that, once people get elected to either the US House or Senate, they think they own those jobs and build political bases back home in hopes of being reelected, thus becoming part of what Donald Trump called the Washington, DC, swamp.

American citizens have been complacent for too long about the workings of their government and Congress. They have come to the realization that the legal system is out of control and the minions on the police forces are forced to carry out the mistakes made. Many citizens have no idea that Congress members can retire with the same pay after serving only one term, that they do not pay into the Social Security system, and that they specifically exempted themselves from many of the laws they have passed (such as being exempted from any fear of prosecution for sexual harassment), while the average American citizen must live under those laws. The latest congressional trickery involved congresspeople attempting to exempt themselves from the national health care reform bill that was passed by the Obama-Biden administration, in all its forms.

Somehow, all this does not seem logical or appropriate. We do not have elite individuals who are above the law, such as Congress members or righteous bigots (or we *should* not) running this country. The author of this book could not care less if they are Democrats, Republicans, Libertarians, progressives, independents, neoconservatives, or whatever. This self-serving, overrighteous concept of our lawmakers must stop immediately. It is bankrupting the nation, just like the out-of-control American judiciary and the career politician have ruined the country. Reform is long overdue, and its time has finally come. The proposed twenty-eighth amendment (since we have made twenty-seven amendments already) is a good way to change the damage done by the out-of-control judiciary and self-serving career politicians.

What Is the Twenty-Eighth Amendment?

The proposed twenty-eighth amendment to the US Constitution, as perceived by the author of this text, states that Congress members should realize that their self-serving interests, lifetime appointments to the Supreme Court, and career politicians have resulted in harmful manifestations to the ideals of democracy, leading the United States of America to a socialistic-oligarchical form of government.

Term limits on congress members and court justices need immediate attention. Additionally, the following text should be part of the amendment:

> Congress shall make no law that applies to the citizens of the United States but does not apply equally to the members of Congress themselves, and Congress shall make no law that applies to the senators and representatives and does not apply equally to the citizens of the United States

of America. Lifetime appointments to any federal position (legislative branch, executive branch, or judicial branch) shall be completely abolished from the Constitution, as well as judicial immunity for lawmakers.

The proposed twenty-eighth amendment, or the so-called Congressional Reform Act of 2011, will address several issues.

Term Limits and Position Requirements for Supreme Court Justices

- Supreme Court justices on both federal and state levels will no longer be appointed for life.
- Supreme Court justices on both federal and state levels will be chosen in free and open elections (the same criteria for training and experience as already used will apply) with a set sum of money allowed to be spent on campaigning, with no overages.
- Supreme Court justices on both federal and state levels can serve for only an eight-year term and will not be allowed to rerun for a second term. Retirement and base pay will be adjusted for eight years only, not made on a lifetime appointment basis.

Term Limits and Conditions on Congress Members

- Congress members will serve only six-year terms (in an attempt to remove career politicians, such as the Ted Kennedy dynasty in Massachusetts and the Harry Reid dynasty in Nevada). Possible alternatives below should be considered:
  o One six-year Senate term
  o Three two-year House terms
  o For any one politician, one six-year Senate term and three two-year House terms. Do not be duped into believing that experience leads to better representation; history has clearly shown that experience leads to more legislative "pork" and outright corruption due to seniority control.
- Congress members will not have tenure or a specialized pension fund.

- o A Congress member collects a meager salary while in office and receives no special pension fund or pay when they are out of office.
- Congress (past, present, and future) participates in the public Social Security system just like all Americans. All funds in the current plush congressional retirement fund must be moved to the Social Security system immediately. All future funds flow into the Social Security system, and Congress participates with the American people they are elected to govern. Also, payouts of Supplemental Security Income (SSI) to individuals who have not paid into the Social Security system are abolished.
- Congress members will, like all other Americans, have the option to purchase retirement plans available to anyone.
- Congress members will no longer vote for pay raises for themselves. Congressional pay will be linked to the Consumer Product Index (CPI) and will rise with the lowering of CPI, with 2.5 percent as the maximum.
- Congress members will lose their current plush health care benefits, which are not available to common Americans. Congress members will be forced to participate in the same national health care system as all other Americans, whether they like it or not.
- Congress members must equally abide by all laws past and future that they approve. They will get no special exemptions or treatment for being present or former Congress members.
- All lobbyist contracts with past and present Congress members for special treatment are null and void, effective January 1, 2012, or at least have a specified and definite ending date set.
- An agreed ceiling should be placed on time and money spent by political action committees (PACs) on individual Congress members, or if no agreement for a ceiling can be reached, then initiate plans to outlaw PACs completely.
- The Congress members, as representatives of the federal government, will be required to tell the American people the "plain truth" that, despite the fact that the US Constitution was enshrined as the supreme law of the land, it does not run things, as the Unified Commercial Code (UCC) designed and implemented

by the American Bar Association does. (Google "UCC" to learn how it controls everything.)

Term Limits to Remove Career Politicians

The proposed twenty-eighth amendment to the US Constitution, outlined above with some modifications (sometimes circulated in modified form as the Congressional Reform Act of 2011), suggests that all laws made by Congress applying to citizens of the United States apply equally to members of Congress themselves, a sentiment that is commonly expressed by critics of retirement benefits and health reform efforts, and that the stagnated Supreme Court systems on both state and federal levels are the way they are because of lifetime appointments. Communicating this message all across the nation will require a few considerations:

- This sounds like a great idea, but further explanation is required to explain options of how these changes can come about.
- It will require massive communication to get the word out, and the existing bar associations will be fighting the message all the way.
- For example, each person could contact a minimum of twenty people in their email contacts, and in turn, each of those does likewise.
- In about three days, with the speed and widespread use of the free international internet, all the people in each state, as well as the overall union, will have the message.
- This is one proposal that really should be passed around and ultimately implemented, despite the out-of-control legal system and career politicians.

This is a saving-grace idea to save democracy in America—an honest attempt at removing the greed for wealth and power in government. In most states, agreement among only three-fourths of the state legislature is required to pass a proposal into law, and these laws should be written to specify that they are veto-proof, *including no appeals to the Supreme Court*, which would surely shoot the proposals down. Let us get the word out to every red-blooded American. Congress and the out-of-control court systems have brought this upon themselves with their greed for control, power, and money! Think of the money that will be saved; and with a reduction in PACs and lobbyists, problems will be solved more quickly! Savings associated with national public health care, Medicare and Medicaid, Social Security, IRAs, pension plan reform, and on and on will increase. The American people did not make greed contracts with Congress members when they were elected. Congress members were essentially greedy for money and made many contracts with PACs and lobbyists for their own ill-gotten gain and get-rich-quick schemes. The American people must get back to the original Founding Fathers' *idea*—that is, serving in Congress is an *honor*, not a career. The Founding Fathers envisioned citizen legislators, so ours should serve their terms, go home, and get back to work. The Founding Fathers had no vision at all about career politicians; that is *just an insidious evil* that has evolved over two-hundred and twenty years and that needs to be *eliminated with the proposed twenty-eighth amendment.* The fact of the matter is that the twenty-eighth amendment has been brewing in the minds of Americans for some time now.[1]

Supreme Court Justices Should Not Get Lifetime Appointments

The original proposed twenty-eighth amendment did not mention Supreme Court justices, who are appointed for life (big mistake as time has proven). This author thinks that a rider should be attached to the original proposal with no appeal rider for Supreme Court justices specifying the following:

- Lifetime appointments are terminated immediately. Presidents will not get to make future appointments, and when a vacancy occurs, presidents will set things in motion for a replacement.
- Supreme Court justices can serve a maximum of sixteen years maximum.
- All individuals seeking a Supreme Court position will no longer be appointed by the president and will have to pay filing fees and campaign just like those who wish to be US senators or

representatives, as a safeguard against packing the court with liberals or conservatives. Let the people decide with an honest election.

- The Supreme Court will keep nine members, consisting one chief justice and eight regular justices.
- No appeal clause will be inserted to prevent any attempts in the future to expand number of the Supreme Court members.
- Filing fees, campaign time periods, and maximum amounts of money to spend on campaigns will be set by Congress sometime in the future.
- Also, strongly stipulate that, *in all US elections,* only US-made voting machines will be used, along with US-designed software running on a secure US-designed *intranet that is not subject to internet attacks from foreign servers on the internet.*[2]

Summary

Although these items could be said to have no real true or false quality (since they are just hypothetical proposals), the author considers them mostly true because the supporting arguments they put forward are all true. Common answers to the following questions put forth are all positive:

- *Is this [text] the actual twenty-eighth amendment to the US Constitution?*

Yes, with the exception of the addition of term limits on Supreme Court justices on both the state and federal levels and the federal government coming clean and being honest with the American people. Note: The US Constitution has been amended twenty-seven different times, the last of which (a limit on congressional pay increases) was ratified in 1992. This item is a proposed twenty-eighth amendment only in the very loose and simplistic sense that it advocates any change to the US Constitution. It is rather unlikely that such a broadly worded amendment could pass because of the self-regulated and self-serving judicial system, yet it must be ratified by all states to even come up for a vote on the floor of Congress itself.

- *Could this amendment be passed without Congress's voting on it?*

Yes and no. Article 5 of the US Constitution specifies two procedures for amendments. One method is for two-thirds of state legislatures to call for a constitutional convention at which new amendments may be proposed, subject to ratification by a three-fourths majority of the states. The constitutional convention method allows for the Constitution to be amended by the actions of states alone and cuts Congress out of the equation—no congressional vote or approval is required. However, not once in the history of the United States have the states ever called a convention for the purpose of proposing new constitutional amendments. The other method for amending the Constitution (the one employed with the past twenty-seven amendments so far proposed or enacted) requires that the proposed amendment be approved by both houses of Congress (i.e., the Senate and the House of Representatives) by a two-thirds majority in each and then ratified by three-fourths of the states. It is probably safe to say that the odds that a supermajority of both houses of Congress would pass an amendment that takes away the self-regulation of the judiciary and places such restrictions upon themselves (Congress members) are very low indeed.

- *Can members of Congress retire with full pay after serving only a single term?*

Yes! This is a long-standing thorn in the backside of the American people that was embedded in the fine print and apparently approved with the twenty-seventh amendment to the Constitution in 1992. It should be repealed.

- *Are members of Congress exempt from paying into Social Security?*

Yes! Similar to all federal employees, although Congress members initially participated in the Civil Service Retirement System (CSRS), rather than Social Security, since 1984 all members of Congress have been required to pay into the Federal Retirement System or into their own retirement system, which is completely separate from the Social Security system, while all other working Americans are automatically forced to participate in it without any options.

- *Are members of Congress exempt from prosecution for sexual harassment?*

Yes! The passage of Public Law 104-1 (the Congressional Accountability Act of 1995, also known as CAA) made a variety of laws related to civil rights and workplace regulations applicable to the legislative branch of the federal government. Section 1311(a) of the CAA specifically prohibits sexual harassment (as well as harassment on the basis of race, color, religion, or national origin). However, some fine print in the law exempted long-term Congress members; a required proof of accusation has to be made before charges can be filed (this was not characteristic of others). In other words, seniority was protected, and freshmen Congress members were open game.

- *Did members of Congress try to exempt themselves from current national health care reform legislation?*

Yes! This claim is based on the fact that congressional efforts to establish a "public option" for health insurance (originally designed to protect federal health care programs that were much cheaper and better than those programs offered to the general public) would have required everyone except members of Congress to participate in a new federal insurance plan. The proposed legislation would have required everyone, including members of Congress, to have health insurance that met minimum benefit standards and, to that end, called for the creation of insurance exchanges that would offer health plans to those who could not otherwise afford insurance plans that met the minimum-benefits criteria. The members of Congress were very clever. They still got their plush federal health care system protected in the end. In fact, the final version of the health care reform legislation that was eventually passed in March 2010 stated that "members of Congress and congressional staff" will only have access to plans that are created by the health care bill or offered through the exchange established by the bill. Nothing in the bill, however, prevented the exchange from creating something for the members of Congress or its staff members with federal strings attached that were not available to the general public.

According to the bill, members of Congress in the exchange:

- Requirement—Notwithstanding any other provision of law, after the effective date of this subtitle, the only health plans that the federal government may make available to members of Congress and congressional staff with respect to their services as members of Congress or congressional staff shall be health plans that are:
  - created under the act (or amendment made by this act), or
  - offered through an exchange established under this act (or an amendment made by this act).

It is highly suspected that, with this open-ended verbiage in the law, many states will refuse to accept federal funding for the exchange program, and no workable national health care reform will take place any time soon (we hope).

However, there is a real need for this proposed twenty-eighth amendment to the US Constitution. Most people consider it to be merely a bit of internet politicking and not something that is serious or should be introduced or proposed as a potential amendment by any current member of Congress. Somehow, the JAIL (Judicial Accountability Initiative Law) bill should be attached (as a sneaky lawyer trick) as a rider to the twenty-eighth amendment to ensure the ending of judicial improprieties for good and some control.[3]

Now, please proceed to the next chapter to learn about the numerous failures of big government (CDC, in particular) in the handling of the pandemic crisis and the attempt to eradicate COVID-19, which was an *accidental bioweapon attack from the Wuhan Institute of Virology in China that affected the entire globe (according to the Chinese when the truth finally came out).*

CHAPTER 10

✳ ✳ ✳ ✳

CDC (BIG GOVERNMENT) KNOWS BEST REGARDING THE CONTROL OF BIOWEAPONS THAT CAUSE PANDEMICS AND DEATH IN THE COUNTRY

It is said that we have the best government
the world ever knew, and I am glad to meet
you, the supporters of that government.
— Abraham Lincoln

Let us review the facts that are now known about the coronavirus (COVID-19) pandemic that spread all over the globe:

- The Centers for Disease Control and Prevention (CDC) was given the responsibility to stop the spread but did not.
- Small businesses went under because customers were under lockdowns.
- President Trump launched Operation Warp Speed to quickly develop a vaccine.
- Travel among countries was restricted.
- Overall panic was everywhere as people were dying.
- Lockdowns were instituted to attempt to control the spread.
- Social separation was initiated to halt the spread.

- Travel anywhere was discouraged, and people who did travel had to wear masks.
- Large gatherings of people were suspended.
- Businesses with over a hundred employees were mandated to have vaccinated staffs.
- People were required to wear masks in public.
- Aircrafts, buses, and trains required all passengers to wear masks twenty-four seven.
- CDC called it a pandemic when, in reality, it was an accidental release of a bioweapon from the Wuhan Institute of Virology in China, which they still deny today.

All the items mentioned above almost resulted in an economic crash in many places across the globe. In the race to defeat the pandemic, countries rolled out their vaccination programs. Vaccines from various companies—Pfizer (US), Johnson & Johnson (US), Moderna (US), Oxford-AstraZeneca (UK), Sputnik V (Russia), and Indian Covaxin and Covishield—were created as every country was striving to be rid of COVID-19 as quickly as possible. Besides the expected results, the vaccines have been under scrutiny since phase 1 of the trials.[1]

Pro and Cons of COVID-19 Vaccinations

Every nation is desperate to return to normalcy after being punched in the guts by the pandemic. With the UK's tightening its rules, India's loosening up a little, and New Zealand's securing its perimeter, these pros and cons of COVID-19 vaccines evaluate the current and future scenario globally.

COVID-19 Vaccination—Pros

- **Immunity boost:** Beyond just COVID-19, the vaccine promises to work against other immuno-deficiency diseases, including the common flu. The biggest advantage of the COVID-19 vaccine is that it creates an antibody response in recipients' bodies without their becoming infected with the novel coronavirus. Best of all, even if they are infected, the vaccine will prevent coronavirus complications.

- **No more staying at home:** Now, at least the people getting the vaccine can walk out of their homes knowing they are immune to the airborne virus. Mobility has been a major concern among people locked inside their houses. Apart from all the problems, people faced real concerns about staying inside while overlooking their essential needs.

- **Job opportunities:** According to the Pew Research Center, America alone had 20.5 million jobless people due to the coronavirus within three months. With countries' trying to rebuild their economies, people's job opportunities increased. Getting vaccinated is one way individuals can get back basic freedoms and walk out to search for jobs.

- **Travel:** The biggest benefits of the COVID-19 vaccine will be to those who travel frequently. Private organizations have already started working on mandating shots for those who have to take flights, vacation on cruise ships, or attend business events. The governments will continue the travel ban as expected, but the norms are expected to change after most people are vaccinated.

COVID-19 Vaccination—Cons

- **The delay:** Consider how long it will take to provide a vaccine to every single citizen. The time taken in research, development, manufacturing, and distribution adds insult to injury, not to mention that recombinant mRNA vaccines had not been fully approved as safe. The delay in vaccinating everyone would be stark enough to let the contagion spread further. Although some vaccines provide 95 percent security against the disease, the world is expected to witness more casualties in the coming times.

- **Interaction with existing medications:** Every vaccine comes with some sort of side effect as people's immune systems responds to it. As per CDC reports, the most common side effects of the COVID-19 vaccine include pain and swelling, and people may also experience fever, chills, fatigue, and headache. These issues may persist for a long time if the recipient is undergoing medical treatment for chronic ailments. The side effects may also vary from person to person.

- **Efficacy concerns regarding mutated COVID-19 (so-called variant strains):** Reports of COVID-19 mutation in the UK raised many concerns among researchers as they were not prepared to tackle the new variant. Also, multiple variants of the COVID-19 virus were documented in the United States and globally during the pandemic. According to some reports, multiple variants of the virus that causes COVID-19 circulated in the UK, Russia, and Brazil.

- **Efficacy concerns regarding patients with chronic illness:** The vaccine's positive effect is still under study as chronic patients might show zero or little response to it. The COVID-19 vaccine seems to be less effective in people with inflammatory bowel disease. Much to the world's surprise, South Africa suspended the use of AstraZeneca's COVID-19 vaccine after finding that it failed to stop coronavirus variants. Yet scientists are hopeful that it might still prevent severe disease and fatalities. Since the vaccination program is still under trial, more is expected after the third phase. It was reported that people who were diabetic and over sixty-five years of age and also got a recombinant mRNA vaccine had a 50 percent chance of dying because of their already strained immune systems.[2]

CDC Is Not Designed to Handle Bioweapon Attacks and Made Huge Mistakes

The CDC's many mistakes could have been predicted as it is an agency designed to control and prevent the spread of diseases, not to handle bioweapon attacks from other nations, which is primarily a military responsibility. The release of the coronavirus from the Wuhan Institute of Virology in China is now viewed as an accidental release of a bioweapon on the entire globe—let us call it what it really was. The pandemic (bioweapon attack) was a test of America's public-health bureaucracy, and it failed big time. Those failures were legion, and they were spread across multiple officials, agencies, and layers of government. But no institution failed quite as abysmally as the CDC, which, through a combination of arrogance, incompetence, and astonishingly poor planning, wasted America's only chance to mitigate the effects of COVID-19 before it spread widely. Following are the most awful mistakes that were made:

- **Downplaying the danger and sidelining experts.** During the pandemic's crucial early days and weeks, then president Donald Trump and other authority figures actively minimized the virus's threat. Trump dismissed it as no worse than the flu and said the pandemic would be over by Easter. (He attempted to stop a panic but left the public guessing.) The CDC initially told the media that the threat to the American public was low. When a CDC spokesperson acknowledged in late February that disruptions to daily life could be "severe," the agency was quickly sidelined—and Trump himself became the government's main conduit for COVID-19 updates through his daily briefings. This muzzling of the CDC and top government health experts made it hard for them to communicate accurate and lifesaving scientific information to the public. Under President Joe Biden's administration, government science agencies and health officials have been given renewed respect and independence. But rebuilding public trust in these authorities will still take time.

- **Slow and flawed testing.** The CDC developed its own test for the virus rather than employing a German-developed one used by the World Health Organization (WHO). But the CDC test was flawed, causing a deadly delay while scientists worked out the problem. The agency was not designed to produce tests at the scale needed to spot the infections as they silently spread through the population. Meanwhile, the Food and Drug Administration was slow to approve tests made by private companies, as reported by the Johns Hopkins Center for Health Security. They also said the earliest criteria for getting a test were too stringent—one often had to have been hospitalized with severe symptoms and have recently traveled to a "high-risk" area. As a result of these hurdles, the virus spread undetected for weeks. By the time testing became somewhat more available, community spread was already rampant in many places, making it difficult or impossible to do contact tracing and isolate people before they infected others.

- **Inadequate tracing, isolating, and quarantines.** The time-worn methods of combatting an infectious disease—testing people who may be sick, tracing their contacts, and isolating or quarantining those who are positive or exposed—worked for COVID-19 as well. The WHO repeatedly stressed the importance of these measures, and countries that followed this advice closely (such as Vietnam, Thailand, New Zealand, and South Korea) succeeded in controlling their outbreaks. In addition to its test problems, the United States did not do an adequate job of isolating those who were known or suspected to be infected (or had recently traveled to a high-risk area), tracing their contacts, or requiring quarantines for those who were exposed. China imposed extremely strict, city-wide quarantines. Other countries required those who may have been exposed to stay at a government-approved hotel or other facility for a quarantine ranging from a few days to a couple of weeks. Such policies would likely have been harder to implement in the United States, a nation that prides itself on personal freedoms. But not doing so came at the expense of keeping the virus in check.

- **Confusing mask guidance.** Although face masks are now widely considered a crucial part of stopping transmission, US and global health authorities were slow to recommend them for public use. Many countries in East and Southeast Asia, including China and Japan, had normalized mask wearing well before the pandemic— in part because of the SARS outbreak in 2002–2003. Unlike the SARS virus, however, scientists now know that SARS-CoV-2 often spreads before a carrier develops symptoms (and possibly even if they never do). In the early weeks and months of the COVID-19 outbreak, the CDC and WHO stated that face masks were not necessary for the general public unless a person was experiencing symptoms or caring for someone who was. The agencies also initially urged people not to buy high-filtration N95 and surgical masks because they were needed for health care workers and were in short supply because of inadequate government stockpiles. Though perhaps well-meaning, the WHO's and CDC's guidance sent a mixed message about masks' effectiveness—and about who deserves protection. The CDC changed course and recommended cloth face coverings in April. The WHO did not do so until June, citing inadequate evidence of their efficacy before then. The CDC did not respond to a request for comment, and the WHO referred *Scientific American* to press briefings that addressed these issues. In these briefings, experts pointed to a lack of high-quality evidence for mask use. The WHO's director general also stated that, in the absence of other public health measures, "masks alone will not protect you from COVID-19."

- **Airborne spread and "hygiene theater."** Early in the pandemic, US health authorities believed the virus spread primarily by direct contact or relatively large droplets from a nearby cough or sneeze—not by far smaller droplets, called aerosols, that linger in the air. As a result, officials placed a huge emphasis on washing one's hands and cleaning surfaces. Scientists now believe transmission from surfaces is not the main way the virus spreads and that aerosols play a much larger role. Ensuring proper ventilation and wearing well-fitted, high-quality masks are much more effective ways to reduce transmission than deep cleaning surfaces. Yet the latter—which critics have dubbed "hygiene theater"—continues to be a focus of many offices and businesses.

- **Structural racism fueled health inequities.** The pandemic exposed and exacerbated deep-rooted racial and economic inequities in health and health care. Black and Hispanic individuals and other people of color were sickened with, and died of, COVID-19 at disproportionately high rates. Many people in Black and brown communities had already long suffered from high rates of underlying conditions such as obesity and diabetes as a result of inadequate health care, lack of access to nutritious foods and outdoor space, and higher exposure to pollution. They also comprise a large percentage of essential workers in frontline industries with an inherently high risk of COVID-19 exposure, such as nursing homes, meatpacking plants, and restaurant kitchens. The uneven death toll is a wake-up call that far too many people of color lack access to preventative health care, as well as protections such as paid sick leave or hazard pay.

- **Decentralized response.** The US government's structure meant that much of the pandemic response was left up to state and local leaders. In the absence of a strong national strategy, states implemented a patchwork of largely uncoordinated policies that did not effectively suppress the spread of the virus. This caused sudden, massive spikes of infections in many local outbreaks, placing enormous strain on health care systems and leaving no region untouched by the disease. "Every district, every county, every state could make decisions and keep them to themselves," Gandhi says. "And we just have uneven applications of public health recommendations in a way that I can't imagine any other country does." The Trump administration has been widely criticized for how the pandemic played out here. But Gandhi adds that the US government's decentralized nature would likely have been an obstacle under any president.

- **Mandates on businesses.** Companies with more than one hundred employees were mandated to implement mask mandates to prevent spreading of the virus, and these mandates caused a lot of stress.

- **Forced vaccination.** The unproven recombinant mRNA vaccines actually caused some unnecessary deaths themselves. Because of slow communications, people with already compromised immune systems, such as elderly people with diabetes, who were vaccinated had a 50 percent chance of dying from the vaccine itself.

- **Lowering dose for children under six years old.** It now appears this guidance was worthless as deaths in healthy children were very low because they had strong immune systems already.

The root of the problem is the agency's self-conception. It sees itself as the ultimate arbiter of what is true and what to do on all matters of infectious disease. In essence, the CDC believes there is no other authority besides the CDC, so it shuts out private labs from the testing process, insists that its faulty tests actually work pretty well long after problems arise, sticks with overly complicated plans that bog down processes, and resists calls to update its guidance, even when that guidance makes living ordinary life difficult or impossible. In a pandemic, where information is scarce and evolves rapidly—and when hundreds of millions of people have to make decisions right now—the agency's preference for deliberative slowness and absolutist pronouncements would be a problem even if it were largely competent. And as it turns out, the agency isn't that competent at all. At this point, the CDC's cultural dysfunctions are endemic. Given its performance during the pandemic, the agency as we know it today should be scrapped. That isn't politically realistic right now, but at a minimum it should be reformed. Many people want to see a special infectious disease unit modeled after US intelligence services, which are more comfortable with ambiguity and which recognize the need for rapid processing and updating of information that changes rapidly. A CDC that's organized around faster, more humble, more practical forms of information processing would be an improvement. But what we need most is to downgrade the CDC's importance and influence, to focus on distributed systems rather than centralized information hoarding. Among other things, that means a far higher reliance on the private sector. Private labs and manufacturers might have made some mistakes during the test kit development process, but a distributed system wouldn't have been brought to its knees by a single point of failure. The same goes for information distribution and guidelines. Rather than act as if the CDC is the be-all and end-all of wisdom about infectious diseases, officials and individuals should be more open to a variety of less bureaucratic information sources. Indeed, those following various public debates about COVID-19 were reasonably well-informed throughout the process, understanding quickly that it was spread through aerosols, that ventilation was much more important than physical distance, that unmasked outside activity was basically safe, that schools could safely reopen in 2020 with some reasonable precautions. The CDC's pronouncements, meanwhile, were sometimes basically right, sometimes badly wrong, sometimes just muddled—and almost always far too late. The agency's understanding of its role doesn't allow for much systemic self-criticism. But officials who have the authority to demand accountability and reform should do so. And a good place to start is with this book. As always, the first step to healing is diagnosing the disease correctly in the first place.[3–6]

Summary

It is really sad that big government (CDC) had a chance to shine but messed up its handling of the pandemic so badly that many unnecessary deaths occurred—sad indeed. The agency's mistakes are just further proof that big government does not function effectively and that both federal agencies and state agencies need to be downsized. Despite the gradual slowing of the COVID-19 pandemic (really a bioweapon attack), the following question still lingers:

> **What will happen with the new variants?** Several novel strains of SARS-CoV-2 have emerged that could threaten progress against the disease. A variant called B.1.1.7, first identified in the United Kingdom, is deadlier and more transmissible than the original—and it is on track to become the dominant variant in the United States this spring. Another variant that was initially spotted in South Africa, called B.1.351, has mutations that appear to help it to at least partially evade some of the vaccines. A third variant that was first seen in Brazil, called P.1, has overrun parts of that country and also contains worrisome mutations. Currently these variants are in a race with the vaccines, and scientists hope enough people can be vaccinated quickly enough to outmaneuver the new strains. Some vaccine makers are already working on booster shots, should they be necessary.[6]

Now, please advance to the next chapter to learn why having open borders for illegal immigrants with no security is an extremely dangerous protocol to follow in today's terror-infested world.

CHAPTER 11

✳ ✳ ✳ ✳

OPEN BORDERS WITH NO SECURITY

It has long been a grave question whether any government,
not too strong for the liberties of its people, can be strong
enough to maintain its own existence, in great emergencies.
— Abraham Lincoln

No country in the world that is run by a government concerned for the safety and prosperity of its citizenry will have an open border to its country with essentially no security policy regarding immigration. This agenda item on the Democratic platform is another poisonous program designed to eventually destroy America and to gain a large voting base from illegal immigrants entering America.

What Is an Open Border?

According to Wikipedia, an open border is a border that enables free movement of people (and often of goods) between jurisdictions with no restrictions on movement and is lacking substantive border control. A border may be an open border due to intentional legislation allowing free movement of people across the border (de jure), or a border may be an open border due to a lack of legal controls, a lack of adequate enforcement or adequate supervision of the border (de facto). An example of the former is the Schengen Agreement between most members of the European Economic Area (EFTA and the EU). An example of the latter has been the border between Bangladesh and India, which is becoming controlled. The term "open borders" applies only to the flow of people, not the flow of goods and services, and only to borders between political jurisdictions, not to mere boundaries of privately owned property.[1]

Open borders are the norm for borders between subdivisions within the boundaries of sovereign states, though some countries do maintain internal border controls (for example, between the People's Republic of China mainland and the special administrative regions of Hong Kong and Macau, or between the United States and the unincorporated territories of Guam, the Northern Marianas and American Samoa, and the Minor Outlying Islands). Open borders are also usual between member states of federations, though (very rarely) movement between member states may be controlled in exceptional circumstances. Federations, confederations, and similar multinational unions typically maintain external border controls through a collective border control system, though they sometimes have open borders with other nonmember states through special international agreements—such as between Schengen Agreement countries as mentioned above.

Pros and Cons of Open Borders with No Security

Democrats have listed their own conception of pros and cons as referenced to open borders with no security:

Open Borders with No Security—Pros

- It would eliminate the cost of illegal immigration control at national borders.
- Open borders would create temporary illegal immigration opportunities.
- It would improve the flow of illegal immigrants to the country.
- Having open borders would help diversify local economies.
- Open borders help to increase the population base for communities and economics.
- It would encourage more development around the world.

- Higher levels of illegal immigration create lower levels of crime. (In this author's mind, this is definitely not true.)
- Illegal immigration eliminates the employment gaps that exist in the country's economy.
- Open borders immigration could reduce retail prices for consumers in the receiving country.

Open Borders with No Security—Cons

- Open borders could make more people eligible for government assistance, or expand the welfare rolls.
- It would increase competition for available employment opportunities for local citizens who are already present.
- Open borders immigration could create overpopulation problems.
- Some families may struggle to integrate into their new surroundings because of cultural and language differences.
- Open borders immigration would still cause families to split up.
- Immigration from desperation does not guarantee results. (We got a glimpse of this issue in 2017 when 2.2 million people sought asylum throughout Europe and the political fallout from that movement created xenophobia and populism that still impacts society today.)
- Open borders make it much easier for coyotes, international drug cartels, human traffickers, hardened criminals, and terrorists to enter the country.[2]

Build a Wall as One Remedy for the Country's Safety

It is amazing how quickly people (in particular, Democrats) seem to forget that a physical barrier of some kind was approved by the Secure Fence Act of 2006, which authorized a barrier along the southern border of the United States; passed with bipartisan support from twenty-six Democratic senators, including Barack Obama, Hillary Clinton, Joe Biden, and Chuck Schumer; and was signed into law by then president George W. Bush. The fence act included Texas, New Mexico, Arizona, and California. The last remnants of the fence were completed under

President Barack Obama in 2009. Present Donald Trump requested to further expand it, secure funding, and improve the fence that had already received justification and got support because the flow of illegal drugs into the United States across the southern border with Mexico had exploded. Many illegal immigrants are coming into the United States by ground by crossing our southern border illegally, which is bad according to the Texas border patrol agency. They claim that many of these individuals are criminals trying to escape Mexican justice. The question, then, can be raised, "Why would the Democrats want to shut the government down over a barrier they approved?" As a matter of fact, both California and Arizona have built their own walls to control the flow of illegal drugs, and the largest unfenced area remaining is along the Texas border. There were about two hundred miles left to build at the end of the Trump administration, but the new Biden administration stopped the funding. However, the governor of Texas recognized the importance of the project that Trump had started and got approval from the citizens of Texas to complete the remaining two hundred miles of wall.[3,4]

Summary

In summary, this gimmick of the Democratic party regarding open borders with no security as a means of establishing a voters' base is too dangerous to be implemented in today's world. We seem to forget the horrific 9/11 incident when several Saudi Arabian hijackers flew two aircrafts into the twin towers in New York City, creating a horrible incident resulting in the deaths of more than three thousand innocent people. Those hijackers believed in some sort of jihad or holy war against the "Western infidels," and they took action with a mindset that was borderline insanity. This insanity not only killed Americans but caused grief and heartache to people all around the globe who worked in those two buildings or loved someone who did. This terrorist mindset is probably more prevalent today than it was on 9/11, making the world more dangerous than ever. Therefore, no nation (not just the United States) can afford to have open-border immigration in the name of safety screening to protect itself and its citizenry from possible terrorist attacks, which still take place all the time somewhere on the earth. Just watch the national news on any given evening.[5,6]

Now, please proceed to the last chapter of this labor of love and learn about extremisms and why democratic forms of government are doomed to failure after a period of time.

CHAPTER 12

✳ ✳ ✳ ✳

SUMMARY AND CONCLUSIONS

I believe the declaration that "all men are
created equal" is the great fundamental principle
upon which our free institutions rest.
— Abraham Lincoln

We will round out this labor of love on the evils of the far left with a discussion on extremism and how American greed will eventually destroy democratic governments if career politicians are not removed. Finally, this is followed with a summary of how the 2020 election was stolen.

Extremism

According to Wikipedia, extremism is "the quality or state of being extreme" or "the advocacy of extreme measures or views." The term is primarily used in a political or religious sense, to refer to an ideology that is considered to be far outside the mainstream attitudes of society. It can also be used in an economic context when large changes occur. In addition, extreme acts are more likely to be employed by marginalized people and groups who view more normative forms of conflict engagement as blocked for them or biased. However, dominant groups also commonly employ extreme activities (such as governmental sanctioning of violent paramilitary groups or the attack in Waco by the FBI in the United States). Extremist acts often employ violent means, although extremist groups will differ in their preferences for violent extremism versus nonviolent extremism, in the level of violence they employ, and in the preferred targets of their violence (from infrastructure to military personnel to civilians to children). Again, low-power groups are more likely to employ direct, episodic forms of violence (such as suicide bombings), whereas dominant groups tend to be associated with more structural or institutionalized forms (like the covert use of torture or the informal sanctioning of police brutality). Although extremist individuals and groups are often viewed as cohesive and consistently evil, it is important to recognize that they may be conflicted or ambivalent psychologically as individuals or contain difference and conflict within their groups. For instance, individual members of Hamas may differ considerably in their willingness to negotiate their differences with the Palestinian Authority and, ultimately, with certain factions in Israel. Ultimately, the core problem that extremism presents in situations of protracted conflict is less the severity of the activities (although violence, trauma, and escalation are obvious concerns) but more so the closed, fixed, and intolerant nature of extremist attitudes, and their subsequent imperviousness to change.[1]

Why Democratic Governments Usually Fail after a Period of Time

The greed of humankind that strives to contain and to control fellow *homo sapiens* eventually overcomes the most righteous of them all, the politician. A democracy is always temporary in nature (as proven in time); it simply cannot exist as a permanent form of government (with greedy politicians). A democracy will continue to exist up until the time that voters discover they can vote themselves generous gifts from the public treasury and they do just *that* (thus the welfare state is borne by career politicians). From that moment on, the majority always votes for the candidates who promise the most benefits from the public treasury (which is grown by honest hardworking citizenry that actually pay their fair share of taxes), with the result that every democracy will finally collapse due to loose fiscal policy of those in control, which is always followed by a dictatorship (that will survive because of fear and threat of death, powerful control factors). The average age of the world's greatest civilizations has been about two hundred years. (The old Roman Empire evolved from a republic to a democracy, to an oligarchy, to a monarchy, and finally to a total dictatorship that crashed rapidly.)

There are now three camps of which we need to be aware:

1. Those who want to raid the treasury to receive benefits they didn't work for (the politically motivated welfare state pushed by the career politician)
2. Those that feel they should control other people (the career politician)
3. Those with self-control who actually keep things moving in an equitable direction (as in the righteous John Q. Citizen who works and keeps the public treasury solvent and accountable)

If you wish for the longevity of the American democratic form of government (especially for yours and my grandkids), you should become aware of the third camp, follow it, and work toward the following:

1. Downsize both state and federal governments to give the citizenry room to breathe.
2. Do not allow career politicians to evolve as they are the real root to all evil in the American government—in particular, lifetime appointments of Supreme Court justices.
3. Discourage all citizenry from joining the welfare state (which gradually erodes democracies and society in general).
4. Allow free enterprise to flourish with reduced government controls.
5. Advocate term limits on all government officials and in particular Supreme Court justices on both the state and federal levels. (Remember, the career politician is the root of all evil in the American government.)
6. Demand accountability and removal of dishonest public servants. After all, taxpayers have an inalienable right to demand this since they pay these public servants their salaries (which should be as low as possible to discourage the development of career politicians).

7. No longer allow the judiciary to regulate itself, as this has proven to be a monumental mistake over the years—for example, the desecration of the original Constitution and its replacement by the American Bar Association and the judiciary with the Unified Commercial Code is proof enough. *It would be very refreshing to hear these things from those who are running for public office.*

Now, the final summary enlightens readers on the Democratic political party and its plan to push the far-left agenda down the American citizenry's throats.[2]

Summary

For the 2020 election, electors voted on December 14 and delivered the results on December 23. On January 6, 2021, Congress held a joint session to certify the electoral college votes, during which several Republican lawmakers objected to the results and pro-Trump protesters stormed the US Capitol, sending Vice President Pence, lawmakers, and staff running to secure locations. The votes were certified in the early hours of January 7, 2021, by Vice President Pence, declaring Joe Biden the forty-sixth US president. President Biden was inaugurated with Vice President Kamala Harris on January 20, 2021. However, the 2020 election was cleverly stolen by the Democrats, who had planned the steal ever since Donald Trump was elected to the presidency over Hillary Clinton—four years in the making. They used foreign software and foreign Dominion-brand voting machines connected to the internet and subject to alteration by foreign servers, thousands of unverified so-called *universal ballots*, and counting discrepancies in key states such as Arizona, Wisconsin, Georgia, and Pennsylvania. The cover-up of the *Smartmatic foreign-written* software was extremely clever also. The United States was dumb to use foreign voting machines and foreign software that had a secret back door built into it for *data alteration* at the last minute, as was evident with a two-o'clock-in-the-morning, highly weird spike in votes for Joe Biden the night before the announcement of the election results. This has never happened in the past. It is just further proof that some skullduggery was afoot. This was clearly explained by Mike Lindell in two videos called "Absolute Proof" and "Absolute Interference," which everyone should watch. But, unfortunately for the Trump campaign, the Supreme Court justices did not understand how the internet functions, had no idea what backdoor software was, and did not know that using nonverified universal ballots was a mechanism of illegally skewing the outcome. These are the facts, folks, and now the whole country is going downhill due to the incompetence of the Democrats in power and their far-left agenda.[3–8]

However, there is hope on the horizon. As more people learn the evils of the far-left philosophy (the purpose of this book), the chances increase for the United States to design its own voting software and produce its own voting machines connected to its own *intranet, not* the international internet. And in 2024, conservative Republicans can regain control of the country. Make your own call as to whether or not the Democratic party's far-left agenda is or is not *poison* to America. The call is yours.

NOTES

Chapter 1: Introduction

1. Allen, Gary, and Larry Abraham, *None Dare Call It Conspiracy* (Seal Beach, CA: Concord Press, 1972).
2. Jackson, Gaines B., *Run Amuck System (Out of Control American Judiciary)* (Philadelphia, PA: Xlibris Corporation, 2008).
3. ———, *Land of Oppression Instead of Land of Opportunity* (Philadelphia, PA: Xlibris Corporation, 2012).
4. ———, *Indentured Servitude Revisited* (Philadelphia, PA: Xlibris Corporation, 2014).
5. ———, *Rape of the American Constitution by Its Own Government: Political Truth* (Minneapolis, MN: Mill City Press Inc., 2016).
6. ———, *Trump Administration: America's Salvation* (Akron, OH: 48HrBooks Inc., 2019).
7. Chiocchetti, Paolo, *The Radical Left Party Family in Western Europe, 1989–2015* (Ebook ed. London: Routledge, 2016), accessed November 19, 2021, via Google Books.
8. Dunphy, Richard, *Contesting Capitalism? Left Parties and European Integration* (Manchester, England: Manchester University Press, 2004), accessed November 19, 2021, via Google Books.
9. Katsambekis, Giorgos, and Alexandros Kioupkiolis, *The Populist Radical Left in Europe* (Ebook ed., London: Routledge, 2019), accessed November 19, 2021, via Google Books.
10. Kopyciok, Svenja, and Hilary Silver, "Left-Wing Xenophobia in Europe," *Frontiers in Sociology,* vol. 6, no. 2 (June 2021), doi:10.3389/fsoc.2021.666717.
11. March, Luke, and Cas Mudde, "What's Left of the Radical Left? The European Radical Left After 1989: Decline and Mutation," *Comparative European Politics,* vol. 3, no. 1 (April 1, 2005): 23–49, doi:10.1057/palgrave.cep.6110052.

12. March, Luke, "Contemporary Far Left Parties in Europe: From Marxism to the Mainstream?" (PDF), (Berlin, Germany: Friedrich-Ebert-Stiftung, 2008), accessed June 3, 2017, via Library of the Friedrich-Ebert-Stiftung.

13. ———, *Radical Left Parties in Europe* (Ebook ed., London: Routledge, 2012a), accessed November 19, 2021, via Google Books.

14. ———, "Problems and Perspectives of Contemporary European Radical Left Parties: Chasing a Lost World or Still a World to Win?" *International Critical Thought,* vol. 2, no. 3 (September 2012b): 314–339, doi:10.1080/21 598282.2012.706777.

15. McClosky, Herbert, and Dennis Chong, "Similarities and Differences between Left-Wing and Right-Wing Radicals," *British Journal of Political Science,* vol. 15, no. 3 (1985): 331, doi:10.1017/S0007123400004221, accessed January 9, 2022.

16. Gregory, Paul, and Robert Stuart, "The Global Economy and Its Economic Systems" (South-Western College Pub., 2013), 41, 107. Capitalism is characterized by private ownership of the factors of production. Decision making is decentralized and rests with the owners of the factors of production. Their decision-making is coordinated by the market, which provides the necessary information. Material incentives are used to motivate participants.

17. Ibid., p. 107. Real-world capitalist systems are mixed, some having higher shares of public ownership than others. The mix changes when privatization or nationalization occurs. Privatization occurs when property that had been state-owned is transferred to private owners. Nationalization occurs when privately owned property becomes publicly owned.

18. *Macmillan Dictionary of Modern Economics*, 3rd ed., 1986, 54.

19. Bronk, Richard, "Which Model of Capitalism?" *OECD Observer* 1999, no. 221–22 (Summer 2000): 12–15, archived from the original on April 6, 2018, accessed April 6, 2018.

20. Stilwell, Frank. *Political Economy: The Contest of Economic Ideas* (1st ed.) (Melbourne, Australia: Oxford University Press, 2002).

21. Joff, Michael, "The Root Cause of Economic Growth under Capitalism," *Cambridge Journal of Economics*, vol. 35, no. 5 (2011): 873–896, doi:10.1093/ cje/beq054. The tendency for capitalist economies to grow is one of their most characteristic properties.

22. Sanandaji, Nima, "Nordic Countries Aren't Actually Socialist," Foreign Policy, October 27, 2021, accessed April 20, 2022. https://foreignpolicy.com/2021/10/27/ nordic-countries-not-socialist-denmark-norway-sweden-centrist/.

23. Caulcutt, Clea, "The End of the French Left," POLITICO, January 13, 2022, accessed April 20, 2022, https://www.politico.eu/article/ christiane-taubira-last-resort-savior-france-left-tatters/.

24. Flavia Krause-Jackson, "Socialism Declining in Europe as Populism Support Grows," The Independent, December 29, 2019, retrieved April 20, 2022, https://www.independent.co.uk/news/world/europe/socialism-europe-parties-populism-corbyn-left-wing-francois-holland-snp-a9262656.html.
25. Best, Steven, Richard Kahn, Anthony J. Nocella II, Peter McLaren, eds. "Introduction: Pathologies of Power and the Rise of the Global Industrial Complex," *The Global Industrial Complex: Systems of Domination* (Rowman & Littlefield: 2011), xviii.

Chapter 2: More Federal Agencies Are Needed to Quash State Rights

1. "Big Government vs. Small Government: What You Need to Know," Opinion Front, retrieved DATE, https://opinionfront.com/big-government-vs-small-government.
2. DiIulio Jr., John J., "10 Questions and Answers about America's 'Big Government,'" Brookings, February 13, 2017, https://www.brookings.edu/blog/fixgov/2017/02/13/ten-questions-and-answers-about-americas-big-government/.
3. Jackson, Gaines B., "Trump Administration: America's Salvation."
4. ———, "Rape of the American Constitution by Its Own Government: Political Truth."

Chapter 3: Universal Basic Income for All and Legalizing Drugs (Marijuana)

1. Logan Ward, "The Pros and Cons of Universal Basic Income," UNC College of Arts and Sciences, March 10, 2021, https://college.unc.edu/2021/03/universal-basic-income/.
2. "Pro and Con of Universal Basic Income (UBI)," Britannica, February 25, 2021, https://www.britannica.com/story/pro-and-con-universal-basic-income-ubi.
3. Amadeo, Kimberly, "What Is Universal Basic Income?" The Balance, updated August 7, 2022, https://www.thebalance.com/universal-basic-income-4160668.
4. "Should Recreational Marijuana Be Legal?" ProCon.org, updated November 13, 2018, https://marijuana.procon.org/.

5. Kalensky, Melissa, "The Pros and Cons of Medical Cannabis," Clinical Advisor, November 11, 2021, https://www.clinicaladvisor.com/general-medicine/pros-and-cons-of-medical-cannabis-current-evidence/.

6. Kalensky, Melissa, "Cannabis Use Disorder in America," Clinical Advisor, November 12, 2021, https://www.clinicaladvisor.com/home/topics/psychiatry-information-center/cannabis-use-disorder-america/.

7. Sundram, Suresh, "Cannabis and Neurodevelopment: Implications for Psychiatric Disorders," *Human Psychopharmacology*, vol. 21, no. 4 (June 16, 2006): 245–254, https://onlinelibrary.wiley.com/doi/abs/10.1002/hup.762.

Chapter 4: Defund the Police

1. Wikipedia, s.v. "Defund the Police," accessed DATE, https://en.wikipedia.org/wiki/Defund_the_police.

2. Henderson, Howard, and Ben Yisrael, "7 Myths about 'Defunding the Police' Debunked," Brookings, May 19, 2021, https://www.brookings.edu/blog/how-we-rise/2021/05/19/7-myths-about-defunding-the-police-debunk.

3. Ray, Rashawn, "What Does 'Defund the Police' Mean and Does It Have Merit?" Brookings, June 19, 2020, https://www.brookings.edu/blog/fixgov/2020/06/19/what-does-defund-the-police-mean-anddoes-it-have-merit/.

4. Cilizza, Chris, "Even Democrats Are Now Admitting 'Defund the Police' Was a Massive Mistake," CNN, November 5, 2021, https://www.cnn.com/2021/11/05/politics/defund-the-police-democrats/index.html.

Chapter 5: Remove Gun Ownership Period

1. Wikipedia, s.v. "gun control," accessed DATE, https://en.wikipedia.org/wiki/Gun_control.

2. "Gun Control," Gale Opposing Viewpoints Online Collection, accessed DATE, https://www.gale.com/open-access/gun-control.

3. "The Interactive Constitution," National Constitution Center, accessed DATE, https://constitutioncenter.org/interactive-constitution/interpretation/amendment-ii/interps/99.

4. "History of Gun Control," ProCon.org, accessed DATE, https://gun-control.procon.org/history-of-gun-control/.

Chapter 6: Remove Assault Weapons and High-Capacity Magazines

1. "Gun Control," Gale Opposing Viewpoints Online Collection.
2. "Assault Weapons Ban Summary," Dianne Feinstein, accessed DATE, https://www.feinstein.senate.gov/public/index.cfm/assault-weapons-ban-summary.
3. "Carrying Firearms in Your Car or RV W/O a Permit/License," HandgunLaw, accessed DATE, https://www.handgunlaw.us/documents/USRVCarCarry-1.pdf.
4. Schaechter, Judy, "Guns in the Home: Keeping Kids Safe," Healthy Children, accessed DATE, https://www.healthychildren.org/English/safety-prevention/at-home/Pages/Handguns-in-the-Home.aspx.

Chapter 7: Pack the Supreme Court with Left-Minded Judges by Expansion of Members

1. Lord, Debbie, "What Does 'Packing the Court' Mean and Why Are Democrats Talking about It?" Kiro 7, October 9, 2020, https://www.kiro7.com/news/trending/what-does-packing-court-mean-why-are-democrats-talking-about-it/3XACXMDCA5EGNG4WLWU2VLSANE/.
2. Wikipedia, s.v. "judicial procedures reform bill of 1937," accessed DATE, https://en.wikipedia.org/wiki/Judicial_Procedures_Reform_Bill_of_1937.
3. "Pro and Con: Court Packing," ProCon.org, accessed DATE, https://www.britannica.com/story/pro-and-con-court-packing.

Chapter 8: Legitimize the LGBTQ+ Community

1. Wikipedia, s.v. "LGBT community," accessed DATE, https://en.wikipedia.org/wiki/LGBT_community.
2. "LGBT Rights," Human Rights Watch, accessed DATE, https://www.hrw.org/topic/lgbt-rights.
3. GLAAD and Movement Advancement Project, "Talking about Overall Approaches for LGBT Issues," 2011, https://www.lgbtmap.org/file/talking-about-overall-approaches-for-lgbt-issues.pdf.

Chapter 9: Do Not Support the Grass Roots Movement for the Twenty-Eighth Amendment

1. Jackson, Gaines B., "Rape of the American Constitution by Its Own Government: Political Truth," chapter 3.
2. ———, "Trump Administration: America's Salvation."
3. Ibid.

Chapter 10: CDC (Big Government) Knows Best Regarding the Control of Bioweapons That Cause Pandemics and Death in the Country

1. Reiter, Nicholas M., Jennifer G. Prozinski, and Janice P. Gregerson, "The Pros and Cons of Mandatory COVID-19 Vaccinations in the Workplace: Practical Considerations for Employers," June 15, 2021, https://www.venable.com/-/media/files/events/2021/06/the-pros-and-cons-of-mandatory-covid19-vaccination.pdf.
2. "Pros and Cons of COVID-19 Vaccine," MyAyan, accessed DATE, https://www.myayan.com/pros-and-cons-of-covid-19-vaccine.
3. Duerr, Charlie, "Doctors Say the Coronavirus Has Ruined the CDC's Reputation," BestLife, June 4, 2020, https://bestlifeonline.com/coronavirus-ruined-cdcs-reputation/.
4. Larsen, Andy, "Where the CDC Went Wrong on COVID-19 Spread, Masks, and Vaccination Benefits," May 13, 2021, https://www.sltrib.com/news/2021/05/13/andy-larsen-biggest/.
5. Suderman, Peter, "The CDC Made America's Pandemic Worse," Reason, September 23, 2021, https://reason.com/2021/09/23/the-cdc-made-americas-pandemic-worse/.
6. Lewis, Tanya, "How the U.S. Pandemic Response Went Wrong—and What Went Right—During a Year of COVID," Scientific American, March 11, 2021, https://www.scientificamerican.com/article/how-the-u-s-pandemic-response-went-wrong-and-what-went-right-during-a-year-of-covid.

Chapter 11: Open Borders with No Security

1. Wikipedia, s.v. "open border," accessed DATE, https://en.wikipedia.org/wiki/Open-border.
2. "17 Biggest Pros and Cons of Open Borders Immigration," ConnectUs, November 25, 2019, https://connectusfund.org/17-biggest-pros-and-cons-of-open-borders-immigration.
3. "DACA and DREAM Act 101—2017 Update," World Relief, September 7, 2017, https://worldrelief.org/daca-and-dream-act-101-2017/.
4. Jackson, Gaines B., "Trump Administration: America's Salvation," 52.
5. "DACA and DREAM Act 101—2017 Update".
6. Poll, Zoey, "The Case for Open Borders," *New Yorker*, February 20, 2020, https://www.newyorker.com/culture/annals-of-inquiry/the-case-for-open-borders.
7. Krayewski, Ed, "Open Borders in America: A Look Back and Forward," Reason, April 30, 2015, https://reason.com/2015/04/30/open-borders-in-america/.

Chapter 12: Summary and Conclusions

1. Wikipedia, s.v. "extremism," accessed DATE, https://en.wikipedia.org/wiki/Extremism/.
2. Amadeo, Kimberly, "What Is Universal Basic Income?"
3. Jackson, Gaines B., "Why Democratic Governments Fail–Usually after 200 Years," white paper, Republican National Committee, 2020.
4. Lindell, Mike, "Absolute Proof," part 1, YouTube, February 4, 2021, https://video.search.yahoo.com/yhs/search;_ylt=AwrCmrAWmEhjD QgACAwPxQt.;_ylu=Y29sbwNiZjEEcG9zAzEEdnRpZAM Ec2VjA3Nj?p=Absolut+Proof+video&type=0_1000_100_1000_100_2105 23&hsimp=yhs-ext_onelaunch&hspart=reb&ei=UTF-8&fr=yhs-reb-ext_ onelaunch&turl=https%3A%2F%2Ftse2.mm.bing.net%2Fth%3Fid%3 DOVP.vHimecUZ8VlWyjGY_kbW8AEsCo%26pid%3DApi %26w%3D296%26h%3D156%26c%3D7%26p%3D0&rurl=https%3A%2 F%2Ftv.gab.com%2Fchannel%2Frealmikelindell%2Fview%2Fabsolute-proof-601d73a5a5ca1b4ef4f0e602&tit=Absolute+Proof&pos=2&vid= 6e6d4924274c5289c0b6dd4e8f01481c&sigr=kEiaA6Uwl6KY&sigt=LnAu TbkHfOLg&sigi=_sDfxIiqMFsl.
5. Lindell, Mike, "Absolute Proof, Part 2," YouTube, February 6, 2021, https://video.search.yahoo.com/yhs/search;_ylt=AwrCmrAWmEhjDQgABwwPxQt.;_

ylu=Y29sbwNiZjEEcG9zAzEEdnRpZAMEc2VjA3Nj?p=Absolut+Proof
+video&type=0_1000_100_1000_100_210523&hsimp=yhs-ext_onelaunch
&hspart=reb&ei=UTF-8&fr=yhs-reb-ext_onelaunch&turl=https%3A%2F
%2Ftse1.mm.bing.net%2Fth%3Fid%3DOVP.jjmLoYvhhLLHRaORSHyJc
QIID0%26pid%3DApi%26w%3D296%26h%3D156%26c%3D7%26p%
3D0&rurl=https%3A%2F%2Fwww.dailymotion.com%2Fvideo%2Fx7z5tv
f&tit=Absolute+Proof+Documentary+about+Election+by+Mike+Lindell+-+
Part+2&pos=1&vid=bea5b6b162b773359e07a4daf0aac820&sigr=n_OZJ63
WDbto&sigt=m0UqZ1n_2Csl&sigi=x7bsvOEA2HuD.

6. Wikipedia, s.v. "Smartmatic," accessed DATE, https://en.wikipedia.org/
    wiki/Smartmatic.

7. Jackson, Gaines B., "Rape of the American Constitution by Its Own
    Government: Political Truth."

8. ———, "Trump Administration: America's Salvation."

ABOUT THE AUTHOR

Gaines Bradford Jackson, BS, MS, DrPH

D r. Gaines Bradford Jackson has accumulated over twenty years of practical and academic experiences in mathematics and the physical sciences. He received a Bachelor of Science in analytical chemistry from West Texas State University in 1965 and then worked for Sinclair Oil and Gas Company as a plant quality control chemist. In 1972, he received his Master of Science degree in environmental science from the University of Texas at Houston after spending four years in the United States Air Force. Until 1977, he worked for the Oklahoma Department of Health as a wastewater research chemist. In 1983, he received a Doctorate of Public Health in environmental health with an extensive publication on the reuse of primary treated municipal wastewater using the land application technique called the spray run-off method. He has published in numerous national trade journals and invented two workable slide charts—the rectangular "Water Utility Converter" and the circular "Jackson's Water Wheel." He has authored two technical texts, namely "Applied Water and Spent-Water Chemistry: A Laboratory Manual" and "Applied Nomography Training for the Water Utility Operator," and he coauthored with Helen Sue Way (a geologist and professor at St. Gregory's University) "Transitional Science," a two-year curriculum for entry-level college students to enhance their background in basic mathematics, the power-of-ten notation, the metric system, the fundamentals of physical science, the fundamentals of chemistry, and the fundamentals of biology and ecology. Jackson and Way also wrote together the associated hands-on laboratory manual and teacher's guide, with answers to all questions in the original text. Since retiring from thirty-four years of continual academic service at Rose State College, Engineering Science Division, Dr. Jackson has published the following books: *Human Parenting Traps; An Academic Plan for Success Known as the Pentagram Spectrum of Success; Run Amuck System (Out of Control American Judiciary); How to Save a Troubled Marriage Biblically; So! You Want to Study Chemistry: What You Need to Know; Land of Oppression Instead of Land of Opportunity; Life's Survival Kit; Rape of the American Constitution by Its Own Government;* and *The Trump Administration: America's Salvation.* Dr. Jackson is always available for lectures through the Rose State College Retired Professors' Speaker's Bureau in Midwest City, Oklahoma.

ADDITIONAL BOOKS PUBLISHED AND SLIDE CHARTS INVENTED

BY

GAINES BRADFORD JACKSON
B.S., M.S., DR. P.H.

A TREATISE ON THE COMMUNITY HEALTH ASPECTS OF

WATER QUALITY IN CHOCOLATE BAYOU.

by

Gaines Bradford Jackson, B.S.

THESIS

Presented to the Faculty of

The University of Texas

School of Public Health at Houston

in Partial Fulfillment

of the Requirements

for the Degree of

MASTER OF SCIENCE

THE UNIVERSITY OF TEXAS AT HOUSTON

December, 1972

A. **The Master Thesis Done at The University of Texas, School of Public Health, Located at Houston, Texas (1972)**

COLUMBIA PACIFIC UNIVERSITY

GRADUATE COLLEGE

A FEASIBILITY INVESTIGATION TO DEMONSTRATE

THE LAND APPLICATION OF SANITARY WASTEWATERS

UTILIZING THE SPRAY-RUNOFF TECHNIQUE

A DISSERTATION

SUBMITTED TO THE GRADUATE FACULTY

in partial fulfillment of the requirements for the

degree of

DOCTOR OF PHILOSOPHY

BY

GAINES B. JACKSON

Oklahoma City, Oklahoma

1983

B. **The Doctoral Dissertation, That was Later on Published as "Municipal Wastewater Treatment By Overland Flow Method of Land Application," EPA- 60012-79-178, August 1979. (as the research was funded with USEPA Research and Demonstration Grant No. R-803218-06).**

PUBLICATIONS AND INVENTIONS BY GAINES BRADFORD JACKSON BEYOND THE TWO PUBLICALLY PUBLISHED DOCUMENTS OF THE 500 PAGE MASTER'S THESIS AND THE 310 PAGE DOCTORAL DISSERTATION.

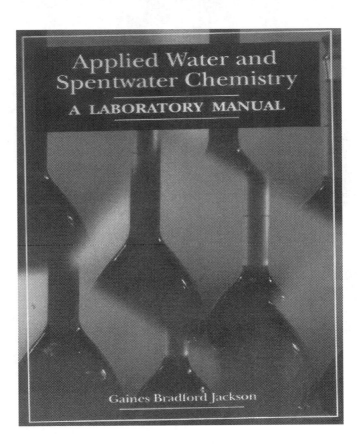

(1.) *"Applied Water and Spentwater Chemistry – A Laboratory Manual."* by Gaines Bradford Jackson, published by **Van Nostrand Reinhold** Publishing Corporation, 115 Fifth Avenue, New York, NY, 1003, (copyrighted 1993), ISBN 0-442-01060-5.

(2.) *"Transitional Science,"* by Gaines B. Jackson and Helen Sue Way, published by **Bellwether-Cross** Publishing Company, 18319 Highway 20 West, East Dubuque, IL. 61025 (copyrighted 2002), ISBN 1-881795-20-9.

(3.) *"Transitional Science – Laboratory Manual,"* by Gaines B. Jackson and Helen Sue Way, published by **Bellwether-Cross** Publishing Company, 18319 Highway 20 West, East Dubuque, IL. 61025 (copyrighted 2002), ISBN 1-881795-21-7.

(4.) *"Applied Nomography Training for The Water Utility Operator,"* By Gaines B. Jackson, published by **Rose Dog** Books, 701 Smithfield Street, Third Floor, Pittsburgh, PA. 15222 (copyrighted 2006) ISBN 10:0-8059-9785-7 and ISBN 13:978-0-8059-9785-9.

(Out-of-Control American Judiciary)

Gaines B. Jackson BS, MS, Dr.PH

(5.) *"Run Amuck System (Out of Control American Judiciary),"* By Gaines B. Jackson, published by **Xlibris** Corporation, International Plaza II, Suite 340, Philadelphia, Pennsylvania, 19113 (copyrighted 2008), ISBN 978-4363-5058-7.

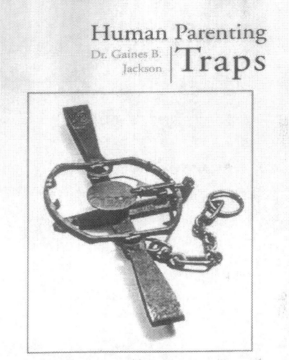

Human Parenting
Dr. Gaines B. Jackson | Traps

An Educational Training Manual

(6.) *"Human Parenting Traps,"* By Gaines B. Jackson, published by **Xlibris** Corporation, International Plaza II, Suite 340, Philadelphia, PA. 19113 (copyrighted 2007), ISBN 978-1-4257-6509-5.

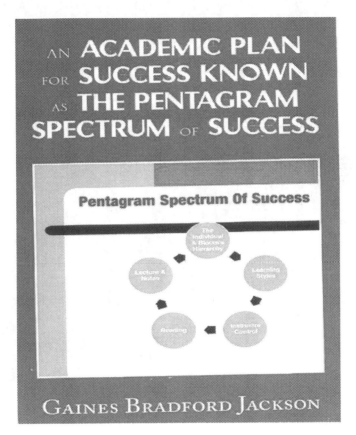

(7.) *"An Academic Plan for Success Known as The Pentagram Spectrum of Success"* By Gaines B. Jackson, published by **Xlibris** Corporation, International Plaza II, Suite 340, Philadelphia, Pennsylvania, 199113 (copyrighted and published in 2009), ISBN 978-1-4415-0913-0.

HOW TO SAVE A
TROUBLED
MARRIAGE BIBLICALLY

GAINES BRADFORD JACKSON

(8.) *"How to Save A Troubled Marriage Biblically,"* By Gaines B. Jackson, published by **Xlibris** Corporation, International Plaza II, Suite 340, Philadelphia, Pennsylvania, 199113 (copyrighted and published in 2010), ISBN 978-1-4500-3200-1.

CONTEMPORARY
VIEWPOINTS ON HUMAN
INTELLECT
AND LEARNING

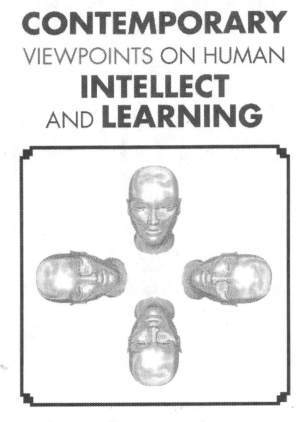

GAINES BRADFORD JACKSON

(9.) *"Contemporary Viewpoints On Human Intellect And Learning,"* By Gaines B. Jackson, published by **Xlibris** Corporation, International Plaza II, Suite 340, Philadelphia, Pennsylvania, 199113 (copyrighted and published in 2010), ISBN 978-1-4568-2160-9.

(10.) *"Land Of Oppression instead of Land Of Opportunity,"* By Gaines B. Jackson, published by **Xlibris** Corporation, International Plaza II, Suite 340, Philadelphia, Pennsylvania, 199113 (copyrighted and published in 2012), ISBN 978-1-4691-7314-6.

(11.) *"Indentured Servitude Revisited,"* By Gaines B. Jackson, published by **Xlibris** Corporation, International Plaza II, Suite 340, Philadelphia, Pennsylvania, 199113 (copyrighted and published in 2014), ISBN -10: 1499019408, ISBN-13: 978-1499019407..

So! You Want To Study Chemistry
What! You Need To Know

Gaines Bradford Jackson

(12.) *"So! You Want To Study Chemistry, What! You Need To Know,"* By Gaines B. Jackson, published by **Xlibris** Corporation, International Plaza II, Suite 340, Philadelphia, Pennsylvania, 199113 (copyrighted and published in 2012), ISBN 978-1-4653-9447-7.

Life's Survival Kit

Gaines Bradford Jackson

(13.) *"Life's Survival Kit"* By Gaines B. Jackson, published by **Outskirts Press Inc.**,10940 South Parker Road 515, Parker. Co. 80134, (copyrighted and published in 2013) ISBN-10: 1478718161, ISBN-13: 978-1478-18161.

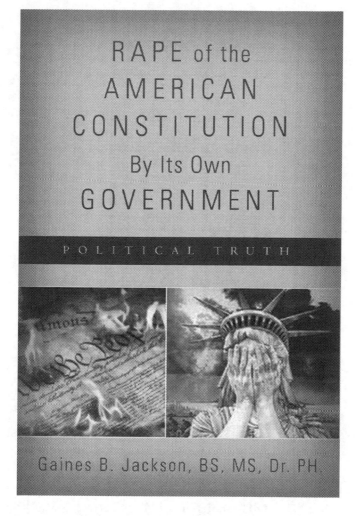

(14.) *"Rape of the American Constitution By Its Own Government –*
Political Truth" by Gaines B. Jackson, Published by **MillCity Press Inc.,**
322 First Ave North, Suite 500, Minneapolis, Mn. 55401, (copyrighted and
published in 2016), ISBN-13: 978-1-63413-998-4, LCCN: 2016909037.

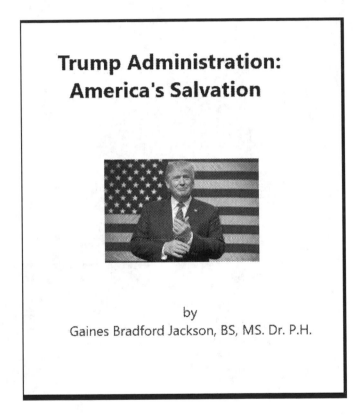

**Trump Administration:
America's Salvation**

by
Gaines Bradford Jackson, BS, MS. Dr. P.H.

(15.) *"Trump Administration: America's Salivation"* by Gaines B. Jackson, Published by **48HrBooks Inc.,** 2249 14th Street, S.W., Akron, Ohio, 44314, (copyrighted and published in 2019), ISBN-13:978-0-578-21842-7.

TWO WORKABLE SLIDE CHARTS INVENTED BY GAINES BRADFORD JACKSON – ONE RECTANGULAR (WATER UTILITY CONVERTER) AND ONE CIRCULAR (JACKSON'S WATER WHEEL).

Water Utility Converter Explanation Booklet

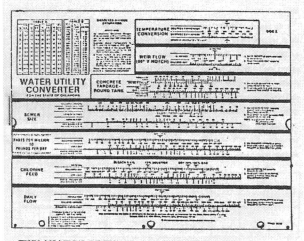

EXPLANATION OF THE MANY SCALES LOCATED ON

THE WATER UTILITY CONVERTER

FALL 1979

SUPPLEMENT FOR THE WATER UTILITY CONVERTER, PREPARED BY GAINES B. JACKSON INSTRUCTOR IN WATER UTILITY TECHNOLOGY, OKLAHOMA WATER UTILITY TRAINING CENTER 6420 S.E. 15TH STREET, MIDWEST CITY, OKLAHOMA 73110

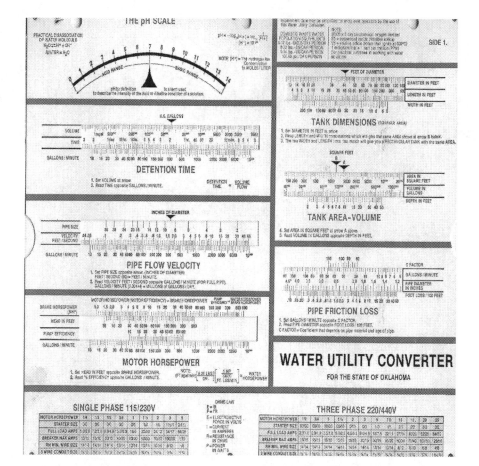

WATER UTILITY CONVERTER

FOR THE STATE OF OKLAHOMA

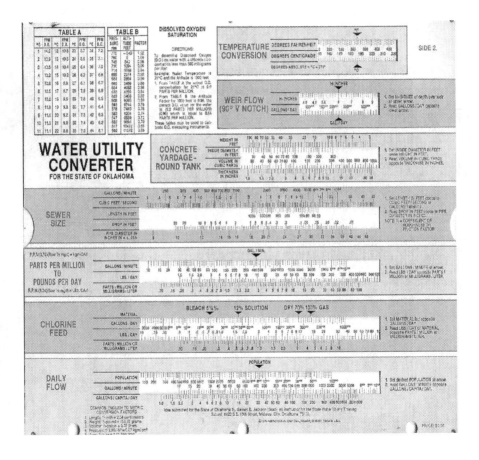

Jackson's Water Wheel

Jackson's Water Wheel
by
Gaines B. Jackson BS, MS, Dr.P.H.
© 2001

TesT Inc. 1250 Three Oaks Circle, Midwest City, OK 73130-5508

Printed in the United States
by Baker & Taylor Publisher Services